thebushtheatre

The Bush Theatre presents the world premiere of

Tinderbox

by Lucy Kirkwood

23 April – 24 May 2008

GW00750245

Cast

John/John Junior Junior/Dixon	**Nigel Betts**
John Junior/Dock/Detective Prawn	**Sartaj Garewal**
Perchik	**Bryan Dick**
Vanessa	**Sheridan Smith**
Saul	**Jamie Foreman**

Director	**Josie Rourke**
Designer	**Lucy Osborne**
Lighting Designer	**James Farncombe**
Sound Designer	**Emma Laxton**
Assistant Director	**Tim Digby-Bell**
Production Manager	**Felix Davies**
Company Stage Manager	**Helen Reynolds**
Deputy Stage Manager	**Rebekah Kirk**
Casting Director	**Chloe Emmerson**

The Bush Theatre would like to thank Pete (the Butcher) Ducksbury, the Tricycle Theatre and Rose Bruford College.

Tinderbox received its world premiere on 23 April 2008.

Nigel Betts
John/John Junior Junior/Dixon

Nigel has worked in theatre all over England including seasons at Bristol Old Vic, York, Cheltenham and the West Yorkshire Playhouse where he played Macduff. One of his favourite roles was playing the title role in *Cyrano De Bergerac* at Lancaster. He has also appeared in the West End and at the National Theatre, recently in the Gunpowder season with the RSC, and just returned from Ireland where he playing leading roles in *The Constant Couple* and *The Recruiting Officer*.

TV includes: *Trial and Retribution*; a semi-regular role in *Emmerdale*; *Coronation Street*; *EastEnders*; *The Bill*; Ray in *The Catherine Tate Show*; *Sharpe*; *Holby City*; *Casualty*; *Midsomer Murders*; *A Touch Of Frost*; *The Inspector Lynley Mysteries*; *Silent Witness*.

Film includes: Philip in *Mrs Ratcliffe's Revolution*; *Thunderpants*; *Paper Mask*; *The Whipping Boy*.

Bryan Dick Perchik

Theatre includes: *Amadeus* (Sheffield Crucible); *The Alchemist, Life of Galileo* (National Theatre); *Lear* (Sheffield); *Bone, Plasticine, Sliding With Suzanne* (Royal Court); *School Play* (Soho Theatre).

TV includes: *He Kills Coppers* (Ecosse TV); *The Old Curiosity Shop* (Curiosity TV); *Sold, Torchwood* (DW Productions); *Miss Marple* (Granada); *Vincent* (Granada); *Shameless* (Company Productions); *Elizabeth the Virgin Queen, Bleak House* (BBC).

Film includes: *Blood and Chocolate* (Lakeshore Entertainment); *Brothers of the Head* (Marlin Films Ltd); *Master and Commander on the Far Side of the World* (Twentieth Century Fox).

Jamie Foreman Saul

Theatre includes: *The Front Page, The Cherry Orchard* (National Theatre); *Irish Eyes English Tears* (Royal Court); *Killing Time* (Croydon Warehouse); *London's Calling, Thick As Thieves* (Stratford East).

TV includes: *Spartacus, Hustle, Doctor Who* (BBC); *The Last Detective, Family* (ITV); *Family Business* (Tiger Aspect).

Film includes: *Hippie Hippie Shake* (Universal Pictures); *Out There* (White Light Films); *Inkheart* (NewLine Cinema); *The Grind, Matchstalk Man, Thirteen* (Silver Pictures/Opex Films); *Oliver Twist, Layer Cake* (Sony Pictures); *Football Factory* (Kickback Productions); *I'll Sleep When I'm Dead* (Will & Co Productions); *Nil By Mouth* (SE8 Group); *Gangster # 1* (No. 1 Films); *Elizabeth* (Polygram).

Sartaj Garewal
John Junior/Dock/Detective Prawn

Theatre includes: *Little India* (Trestle); *The Hot Zone* (BAC); *Too Close To Home* (Lyric Hammersmith and national tour); *Romeo and Juliet* (Royal Exchange); *East Is East* (New Vic, Stoke); *Taming of the Shrew* (Arcola); *London Continental* (Arcola and London tour); *Villette* (British Library); *Ashes to Ashes* (Tristan Bates and Edinburgh Festival); *Tirant Lo Blanc* (Bridewell); *The Tale of the Sleeping Mummy* (Southwark Playhouse); *Candide* (Lost Theatre).

TV includes: *Casualty, EastEnders*, Marvin Dale in *Doctors* (BBC); *Dirty War* (BBC/HBO); *Keen Eddie* (Paramount TV); *The Bill* (Talkback Thames).

Film includes: *The League of Extraordinary Gentlemen* (Twentieth Century Fox); *Cats and Trees* (Liquidamber Films); *Christie* (Motion Picture House); *Ladders* (Rathouse Films).

Radio includes: regular role of Kuljit in *Silver Street* (BBC); *The Spiritual Centre, The Verb* (BBC Radio 3); *The Archers, Claire in the Community* (BBC Radio 4).

Sheridan Smith Vanessa

Theatre includes: *Into the Woods* (Donmar Warehouse); *Ancient Lights* (Hampstead); *The People are Friendly* (Royal Court); *The Taming of the Shrew, A Midsummer Night's Dream* (Regents Park Open Air Theatre); *Little Shop of Horrors* (Menier Chocolate Factory), for which she received an Olivier Award nomination.

TV includes: seven series of the hugely successful BBC series *Two Pints of Lager and a Packet of Crisps; Grown Ups, Love Soup, The Lenny Henry Show, Eyes Down, Doctors, Holby City, The Royle Family* (BBC); *The Bill* (Talkback Thames); *Whitby Royal, Fat Friends* (Tiger Aspect); *Blood Strangers* (Granada); *The Comic Strip Presents Sex Actually*.

Radio includes: *Doctor Who* (BBC).

James Farncombe Lighting Designer

Work at The Bush includes: *the dYsFUnCKshOnalZ!*, *Crooked*, *I Like Mine With a Kiss*.

Other theatre includes: *Taking Care of Baby*, *Osama the Hero*, *A Single Act*, *Life After Scandal* (Hampstead); *Breaking the Silence*, *Beast on the Moon* (Nottingham Playhouse); *Three Sisters* (Birmingham Rep); *Vincent in Brixton*, *The Glass Menagerie* (New Wolsey, Ipswich); *Be My Baby* (Stoke New Vic); *We That Are Left* (Watford Palace); *Touch Wood* (Stephen Joseph, Scarborough); *Blonde Bombshells of 1943* (Hampstead/TEG Productions). James lives in South London, on a hill.... For production photographs and a full list of credits, please visit http://web.mac.com/jamesfarncombe.

Lucy Kirkwood Writer

Lucy was born in Leytonstone, attended the University of Edinburgh, and now lives in London. She won the PMA award in 2006 and has since had work performed at the Arcola Theatre, Hackney; the Union Theatre, Southwark; the Latitude festival in Suffolk and by Mind the Gap Theatre Company in New York. She is a writer on the Channel 4 programme *Skins* and is currently resident writer at Clean Break theatre company. *Tinderbox* is her first full professional production.

Emma Laxton Sound Designer

Theatre includes: for the Royal Court, *That Face*, *Gone Too Far!*, *Catch*, *Scenes from the Back of Beyond*, *Woman and Scarecrow*, *The World's Biggest Diamond*, *Incomplete and Random Acts of Kindness*, *My Name is Rachel Corrie* (also Minetta Lane, New York/West End/Galway Festival/Edinburgh Festival), *Bone*, *The Weather*, *Bear Hug*, *Terrorism*, *Food Chain*.

Other theatre includes: *Europe* (Dundee Rep/Barbican Pit); *Other Hands* (Soho); *The Unthinkable* (Sheffield Crucible Studio); *My Dad is a Birdman* (Young Vic); *The Gods are Not to Blame* (Arcola); *Late Fragment* (Tristan Bates).

Lucy Osborne Designer

Lucy graduated from the Motley Theatre Design School.

Work at The Bush includes: *the dYsFUnCKshOnalZ!*, *Artefacts*.

Other theatre includes: *Be My Baby* (New Vic, Stoke); *Some Kind of Bliss* (Trafalgar Studios); *Rope* (Watermill); *Closer* (Northampton Theatre Royal); *Touch Wood* (Stephen Joseph); *Breaker Morant* (Edinburgh Festival 2007); set design on *Ship of Fools* (Theatre503); *The Long and the Short and the Tall* (Sheffield Lyceum and tour); *Dr Faustus* (The Place); *Richard III* (Cambridge Arts); set on *The Tempest* (Box Clever national tour); *The Prayer Room* (Edinburgh International Festival and Birmingham Rep); *Flight Without End*, *Othello*, *Lysistrata* (LAMDA); *Season of Migration to the North* (RSC New Work Festival); *Almost Blue*, which won the Oxford Samuel Beckett Trust Award (Riverside Studios); *The Unthinkable* (Sheffield Crucible Studio); *Generation* (Gate, London).

Forthcoming projects include: *2000 Feet Away*, also for The Bush.

Josie Rourke Director

Josie is Artistic Director of The Bush Theatre. She trained as Resident Assistant Director at the Donmar Warehouse, was Trainee Associate Director at the Royal Court and was Associate Director of Sheffield Theatres.

Directing work includes: *How To Curse* (The Bush); *Loyal Women*, *Crazyblackmuthafuckin'-Self* (Royal Court); *The Cryptogram*, *World Music*, *Frame 312* (Donmar Warehouse); *Believe What You Will*, *King John* (RSC); *The Long and the Short and the Tall*, *Much Ado About Nothing*, *The Unthinkable*, *World Music*, *Kick for Touch* (Sheffield Theatres); *My Dad's a Birdman* (Young Vic); *Romeo and Juliet* (Liverpool Playhouse). She has also directed the 24 Hour Plays at The Old Vic and on Broadway.

Tim Digby-Bell Assistant Director

Tim Digby-Bell left Edinburgh University in 2005. He completed a year's internship with Nica Burns at Nimax Theatres, working on numerous productions in the West End and running a reading of *Rogues* at the Duchess Theatre, starring Christian Slater. He formed Talac Theatre in 2007 and wrote and directed their first production, *Short Stories*, at the Hen and Chickens Theatre. Their second show, *Tell*, which he also wrote and directed, premiered at the Underbelly in the Edinburgh Festival last year, before transferring to the New End Theatre in Hampstead. He is currently writing their next play which will be staged later this year. He has also worked regularly as a comedy scout for the If.Com Awards in Edinburgh.

Other theatre as assistant director includes: *One Flew Over The Cuckoo's Nest* (UK tour, Dir. Tamara Harvey); *Snowbound* (Trafalgar Studios, Dir. Sam Potter).

The Bush Theatre

'One of the most experienced prospectors of raw talent in Europe'
The Independent

The Bush Theatre is a world-famous home for new plays and an internationally renowned champion of playwrights. We discover, nurture and produce the best new playwrights from the widest range of backgrounds, and present their work to the highest possible standards. We look for exciting new voices that tell contemporary stories with wit, style and passion and we champion work that is both provocative and entertaining.

The Bush has produced hundreds of groundbreaking premieres since its inception 36 years ago. The theatre produces up to eight productions of new plays a year, many of them Bush commissions, and hosts guest productions by leading companies and artists from all over the world.

The Bush is widely acclaimed as the seedbed for the best new playwrights, many of whom have gone on to become established names in the entertainment industry, including Steve Thompson, Jack Thorne, Amelia Bullmore, Dennis Kelly, Chloë Moss, David Eldridge, Stephen Poliakoff, Snoo Wilson, Terry Johnson, Kevin Elyot, Doug Lucie, Dusty Hughes, Sharman Macdonald, Billy Roche, Catherine Johnson, Philip Ridley, Richard Cameron, Jonathan Harvey, Conor McPherson, Joe Penhall, Helen Blakeman, Mark O'Rowe and Charlotte Jones. We also champion the introduction of new talent to the industry, whilst continuing to attract major acting and directing talents, including Richard Wilson, Nadim Sawalha, Bob Hoskins, Alan Rickman, Antony Sher, Stephen Rea, Frances Barber, Lindsay Duncan, Brian Cox, Kate Beckinsale, Patricia Hodge, Simon Callow, Alison Steadman, Jim Broadbent, Tim Roth, Jane Horrocks, Mike Leigh, Mike Figgis, Mike Newell, Victoria Wood and Julie Walters.

The Bush has won over one hundred awards, and developed an enviable reputation for touring its acclaimed productions nationally and internationally. Recent tours and transfers include the West End production of *Elling* (2007), the West End transfer and national tour of *Whipping It Up* (2007), a national tour of *Mammals* (2006), an international tour of *After the End* (2005-6), *adrenalin... heart* representing the UK in the Tokyo International Arts Festival (2004), the West End transfer (2002) and national tour of *The Glee Club* (2004), a European tour of *Stitching* (2003), and Off-Broadway transfers of *Howie the Rookie* and *Resident Alien*. Film adaptations include *Beautiful Thing* and *Disco Pigs*.

The Bush Theatre provides a free script-reading service, receiving over 1000 scripts through the post every year, and reading them all. This is one small part of a comprehensive Writers' Development Programme, which includes workshops, one-to-one dramaturgy, rehearsed readings, research bursaries, masterclasses, residencies and commissions. We have also launched a pilot scheme for an ambitious new education, training and professional development programme, **bush**futures, providing opportunities for different sectors of the community and professionals to access the expertise of Bush playwrights, directors, designers, technicians and actors, and to play an active role in influencing the future development of the theatre and its programme.

The Bush Theatre is extremely proud of its reputation for artistic excellence, its friendly atmosphere, and its undisputed role as a major force in shaping the future of British theatre.

Josie Rourke
Artistic Director

At The Bush Theatre

Artistic Director	**Josie Rourke**
General Manager	**Angela Bond**
Literary Manager	**Abigail Gonda**
Bushfutures Co-ordinator	**Anthea Williams**
Finance Manager	**Dave Smith**
Development Manager	**Sophie Hussey**
Marketing Manager	**Dulcie Ball**
Production Manager	**Pauric Hackett**
Chief Technician	**Tom White**
Development Officer	**Sara-Jane Westrop**
Assistant Producer	**Caroline Dyott**
Literary Assistant	**Jane Fallowfield**
Box Office Supervisor	**Ian Poole**
Box Office Assistants	**Kirsty Cox** **Clare Moss** **Alicia Turrell**
Front of House Duty Managers	**Kellie Batchelor** **Adrian Christopher** **Alex Hern** **Abigail Lumb** **Glenn Mortimer** **Lois Tucker**
Duty Technicians	**Adrian Christopher** **Jason Kirk** **Rachel Newson** **Mark Selby** **Shelley Stace**
Associate Artists	**Tanya Burns** **Chloe Emmerson** **Richard Jordan** **Paul Miller** **Lucy Osborne**
Writer in Residence	**Jack Thorne**
Press Representative	**Ewan Thomson & Giles Cooper at Borkowski**
Marketing	**Ben Jefferies at Spark Arts Marketing**

The Bush Theatre
Shepherd's Bush Green
London W12 8QD

Box Office: 020 7610 4224
www.bushtheatre.co.uk

The Alternative Theatre Company Ltd. (The Bush Theatre)
is a Registered Charity number: 270080
Co. registration number 1221968

VAT no. 228 3168 73

supported by

h&f
hammersmith & fulham

ARTS COUNCIL
ENGLAND

Be there at the beginning

Our work identifying and nurturing playwrights is only made possible through the generous support of our Patrons and other donors. Thank you to all those who have supported us during the last year.

If you are interested in finding out how to be involved, please visit the 'Support Us' section of www.bushtheatre.co.uk, or call 020 7602 3703.

Lone Star
Gianni Alen-Buckley
Princess of Darkness
Catherine & Pierre Lagrange

Handful of Stars
Joe Hemani
Sarah Phelps

Glee Club
Anonymous
Judith Bollinger
Jim Broadbent
Clyde Cooper
David & Alexandra Emmerson
Sophie Fauchier
Albert & Lynn Fuss
Piers & Melanie Gibson
Tanny Gordon
Adam Kenwright
Jacky Lambert
Curtis Brown Group Ltd
Richard & Elizabeth Philipps
Alan Rickman
Paul & Jill Ruddock
John & Tita Shakeshaft
June Summerill
The Peter Wolff Theatre Trust

Beautiful Thing
Anonymous
Mrs Oonagh Berry
John Bottrill
Seana Brennan
Alan Brodie
Kate Brooke
David Brooks
Clive Butler
Justin Coldwell
Jeremy Conway
Anna Donald
Mike Figgis
Alex Gammie
Vivien Goodwin
Sheila Hancock
David Hare
Lucy Heller
Francis & Mary-Lou Hussey
Virginia Ironside
The Violet Crème
Kim Lavery
Jeremy and Britta Lloyd

Laurie Marsh
Ligeia Marsh
Kirsty Mclaren
Michael McCoy
Tim McInnerny & Annie Gosney
John Michie
David & Anita Miles
Mr & Mrs Philip Mould
John & Jacqui Pearson
Mr & Mrs A Radcliffe
Wendy Rawson
John Reynolds
Caroline Robinson
David Pugh & Dafydd Rogers
Nadim Sawalha
Barry Serjent
Brian D Smith
Mrs Peter Templeton
Maggie Burrows
Abigail Uden
Barrie & Roxanne Wilson

Rookies
Anonymous
Neil Adleman
Tony Allday
Ross Anderson
Pauline Asper Management
Mr and Mrs Badrichani
Constance Byam Shaw
Tanya Burns & Sally Crabb
Geraldine Caulfield
Nigel Clark
Alan Davidson
Joy Dean
Nina Drucker
Sally Godley
Miranda Greig
Peter Grundy
Sian Hansen
Andy Herrity
Mr G Hopkinson
Joyce Hytner, ACT IV
Robert Israel for Gordon & Co.
Peter James
Hardeep Kalsi
Casarotto Ramsay & Associates Ltd
Robin Kermode
Ray Miles
Toby Moorcroft - Sayle Screen

Georgia Oetker
Mr & Mrs Malcolm Ogden
Julian & Amanda Platt
Radfin
Clare Rich
Mark Roberts
David Robinson
Councillor Minnie Scott Russell
Martin Shenfield
John Trotter
Loveday Waymouth
Clare Williams
Alison Winter

Platinum Corporate Members
Anonymous

Silver Corporate Members
The Agency (London) Ltd
Harbottle & Lewis LLP
United Agents

Bronze Corporate Members
Act Productions Ltd
Artists Rights Group
Hat Trick Productions
Orion Management

Trust and foundation supporters
The John S Cohen Foundation
The Earls Court and Olympia Charitable Trust
The Ernest Cook Trust
Garfield Weston Foundation
The Girdlers' Company Charitable Trust
The John Thaw Foundation
The Kobler Trust
The Martin Bowley Charitable Trust
The Mercers' Company
The Royal Victoria Hall Charitable Trust
The Thistle Trust
The Vandervell Foundation
The Harold Hyam Wingate Foundation

bushfutures

bushfutures is a groundbreaking education, training and development programme that allows emerging theatre professionals and the local community to access the expertise of Bush playwrights, directors, designers, technicians and actors. The programme actively influences future developments at The Bush. We are devoted to finding and nurturing The Bush artists of tomorrow.

Halo Project – August 2008
Come and discover the secret life of Shepherds Bush.
Over five months, emerging performers from Hammersmith and Fulham will work with playwright Simon Vinnicombe to create a new play about The Bush, The Green and the part of London we call home.

bushfutures **Playwrights**
Working with the Literary Department, **bush**futures is developing an exciting and innovative programme to engage emerging playwrights. For 2008, the **bush**futures playwrights project will be **50 Ways to Leave Your Lover.** Written by five remarkable young playwrights, it will tour to Norwich, Oxford and the Latitude festival before performing at The Bush Theatre from July 21 to 26, 2008.

bushfutures **in Schools**
bushfutures develops projects with schools, colleges and tertiary institutions. The Bush is one of Britain's leading New Writing companies. We share our talent and expertise with young people through tailor-made workshops which focus on playwriting, performance and the development of new work.

bushfutures **Associates**
Emerging practitioners make up a group of associates who are an integral part of The Bush community. They are invited to talks and workshops by leading theatre practitioners and involved in development events.

bushtalk
Throughout the year The Bush hosts discussions for the public between leading playwrights and theatre practitioners.

Anthea Williams, **bush**futures Co-ordinator,
bushfutures@bushtheatre.co.uk

TINDERBOX

or, Love Amid the Liver

Lucy Kirkwood

To Pip, Ted, Kirk, Robert and Peggy

Thanks to:

Jeremy Sams, Crofthead Cottage, Deborah Pearson, Humphrey Ker, Penny Pearce and Mikey Moo.

And especially to: Mel Kenyon, Kirsty Coombs, Abigail Gonda, Lucy Osborne and Josie Rourke.

And my parents and White Albert.

I STARTED MAKING MAPS WHEN I WAS SMALL
SHOWING PLACE, RESOURCES, WHERE THE ENEMY
AND WHERE LOVE LAY. I DID NOT KNOW
TIME ADDS TO LAND. EVENTS DRIFT CONTINUALLY DOWN,
EFFACING LANDMARKS, RAISING THE LEVEL, LIKE SNOW.
I HAVE GROWN UP. MY MAPS ARE OUT OF DATE.
THE LAND LIES OVER ME NOW.
I CANNOT MOVE. IT IS TIME TO GO.

Alasdair Gray, Lanark *, 1981*

Characters

PERCHIK, *a tall and thin young man in his mid-twenties, Scottish.*
An Inverness cowboy.
SAUL, *a big, energetic man, sixties or older, old-fashioned*
Cockney accent. He walks with a stick supporting his right leg.
VANESSA, *tired-looking, pretty at one time but this isn't it, thirties*
or older. Noticeable scar down one side of her face.
DIXON
JOHN
WINSTON
JOHN JUNIOR JUNIOR
DOCK
JOHN JUNIOR
DETECTIVE PRAWN

DIXON, JOHN, WINSTON *and* JOHN JUNIOR JUNIOR *are to*
be played by the same actor; as are DOCK, JOHN JUNIOR *and*
DETECTIVE PRAWN.

The play is set in Bradford, Yorkshire, sometime in the twenty-first
century.

Note

(/)   indicates the point that the next speaker interrupts
(–)   indicates an abrupt interruption
(…)   indicates a trailing off
(*)   indicates two or more different characters speaking
        simultaneously

This text went to press before the end of rehearsals and so may
differ slightly from the play as performed.

ACT ONE

'Dry Bones'

The end of a blazing afternoon. An old-fashioned butcher's shop. Tiles, marble slabs, a display counter covered with a sheet. A desiccated feel to the place. A yellowing blind on the window. Straw on the floor. Three dead pot plants and a thriving cactus. The sound of police sirens and dogs barking gets louder and louder. Louder still when the shop door is opened. JOHN *enters. He looks around the empty shop, then calls:*

JOHN. 'Livery!

He mops his brow. He has a stripe of zinc-oxide sunblock on his face and a clipboard in his hand.

Mr Everard? Delivery!

No answer. JOHN *sticks his head out of the door.*

John Junior! You want to stir yer bleedin' stumps, lad?

Beat. Then JOHN JUNIOR *staggers in, dishevelled, and lugging a sack. He also wears sunblock. He dumps the sack and stares accusingly at* JOHN.

(*Innocently.*) What?

JOHN JUNIOR. You left me!

JOHN. I had to see a man about a dog.

During the following, JOHN *takes out a Cornetto and rolls it slowly over his face. He then peels off the wrapper, folds it, puts it in his pocket, and starts to eat.*

JOHN JUNIOR. They were kicking me and you said, 'I'll run ahead and meet you there.'

JOHN. I thought they were your mates.

JOHN JUNIOR. They were trying to set fire to my shoes! (*Beat.*) You know why they always go for me, don't you?

JOHN. You've just got one of those faces, I s'pose.

JOHN JUNIOR. No. It's cos it's always me carrying the bleeding sack!

JOHN. We've been through this, JJ. You carry the sack. I carry the clipboard. See?

He holds up the clipboard to demonstrate.

JOHN JUNIOR. S'like trying to carry a sugar cube through a sea of ants out there! Maybe if you had to be the human donkey once in a while, then – What's that?

JOHN (*still eating*). What does it look like?

JOHN JUNIOR (*gasping in amazement*). It's an ice cream!

JOHN. To some extent.

JOHN JUNIOR. Where d'you get that from?

JOHN (*primly*). Some of us don't fritter away our dairy rations on cheese omelettes, John Junior. Been saving up for weeks for this.

JOHN JUNIOR. Give us a lick.

JOHN. Not on your nelly.

JOHN JUNIOR. Aw, lemme have a –

JOHN. Get off –

JOHN JUNIOR. Just a quick one –

JOHN. NO!

JOHN JUNIOR. Alright, well, what about your wrapper then?

JOHN. What about it?

JOHN JUNIOR. Give us a little suck on it.

JOHN. Piss off.

JOHN JUNIOR. Alright, just a lick then.

JOHN. No. I'm saving it for my wife.

JOHN JUNIOR. I only want a taste, your wife's fat enough already. You're a feeder, you.

JOHN. John Junior! My wife is not fat. My wife has just given birth to a twelve-pound baby, it was a very difficult labour and it's very rude of you to –

JOHN JUNIOR. LET ME LICK YOUR WRAPPER!

JOHN. Pull yourself together, boy! What would Mr Womble say if he could see this exhibition, eh? Now come on. We've got four more drop-offs before we can –

JOHN JUNIOR quickly leans in and takes a big bite of JOHN's ice cream.

You little – !

JOHN JUNIOR runs out. JOHN exits after him. Silence once more. A beat. Another beat. Then the sack bursts open and PERCHIK, choking and spluttering, bursts out. He is blood-streaked. Feathers fly. He leans into the sack and pulls out a knapsack. Quietly, he crosses to the door. Opens it. The sound of a riot; angry crowds, sirens, dogs barking, glass smashing. He slams the door shut again. Suddenly, VANESSA comes running, weeping, through the shop from a door out to the back. She stops short as she sees PERCHIK. They both freeze. Beat.

SAUL (*off*). Vanessa!

VANESSA runs to the icebox door, heaves it open and slams it behind her. PERCHIK panics, jumps back into the sack. SAUL enters hurriedly. He limps on his right foot and carries a stick. He stops and looks at the sack. PERCHIK's heavy breathing can be heard.

(*Under his breath.*) Hmm... fresh.

He runs to the icebox door and bangs on it.

Little pig, little pig, let me come in!

He listens. No reply.

You can't hide in the icebox every time Sauly is naughty, Vanessa.

Pause.

Why won't you play with me?

VANESSA. Go away!

7

SAUL. But Vanessa! I'm having a heart attack! … Ow!

Pause.

OW. (*Beat.*) Really hurts.

Pause. He bangs on the door.

OPEN THIS DOOR!

VANESSA (*singing*). Oh, the toe bone's connected to the foot bone, the foot bone's connected to the –

SAUL. Vanessa!

VANESSA. – *ankle* bone, the ankle bone's connected to the leg bone, the leg bone's connected to the –

SAUL. Shut up!

VANESSA. – *knee* bone, the *knee* bone's connected to the –

SAUL. Open this door now!

VANESSA (*shouting now*). – THIGH BONE, THE THIGH BONE'S CONNECTED TO THE HIP BONE, NOW HEAR THE WORD OF THE LORD –

SAUL. You've left off the torso, you silly cow! If your toes freeze together again, I'm not taking you to the hospital to have them chipped apart this time. I'll do it myself and put the bits in a punch bowl and have cocktails on the bloody veranda!

He waits.

Vanessa?

No response. SAUL goes to the shop door, locks it, and exits. Beat. PERCHIK jumps out of the sack. VANESSA comes out of the icebox. They stare at each other. The power fails.

(*Off.*) I have turned the electricity off, Vanessa!

PERCHIK *and* VANESSA *panic.* PERCHIK *runs and throws himself down behind the counter.* VANESSA *runs to the door, finds it locked, looks around.*

VANESSA (*calling*). Don't be so stupid, Saul. The stock will spoil.

SAUL (*off*). Then you will have that on your conscience, wife.

VANESSA (*calling*). I didn't turn the power off, did I?

SAUL approaches. VANESSA jumps in the sack. SAUL enters. Goes to the icebox.

SAUL. You are behaving in such a naughty way that my hand was forced. Do you understand, wife? You left me no other option. No other option!

Pause. He opens the icebox door and peers in. Closes it silently.

No, no, Vanessa. You're quite right.

SAUL turns to see the sack wriggling across the floor, towards the door. He sighs, goes to the sack and sits on it. It stops moving.

The best thing for us to do is to sit quietly and Think About What You Have Done.

SAUL hacks up some phlegm and spits it into a Union Jack handkerchief.

I am a man of infinite patience. (*He suddenly turns to the counter.*) Whoever you are, I'd come out of there if I was you. The sound of your rattling pipes is getting distinctly on my breasts.

Pause.

I'm talking to you. Behind the counter. It's bloody sardines in here tonight. Come out.

Pause.

Tell you what. Make it sporting. I'll give you till ten. One... two... three... four...

PERCHIK makes a dash for it. SAUL trips him, picks him up and sits him on a chair.

Aha! Can I see your passport please, baggage?

PERCHIK. What? I've no' got a – What? Get off!

SAUL. Ah. You're a *foreign*! Splendid!

PERCHIK. No – I'm Scottish.

SAUL. Like I said. Foreign! Can I see your passport?

PERCHIK. This is an invasion of my civil liberties – What do you want tay see my –

SAUL. An Englishman's home is his castle, but an Englishman's shop is his Empire. We are short on staff at the moment so I am both monarch and border control.

PERCHIK. I don't –

SAUL (*shouting into the sack*). The First Lady has gone AWOL at present.

PERCHIK. I've no' got my passport wimme. I mean – I've no' got a passport.

SAUL. 'No' got a passport'! Dear me. What an untravelled young larrikin you must be. The marvellous crevices of this great turning world are of no interest / to you?

PERCHIK. What are you / on about?

SAUL. Never smelt the swamps of Venice or seen their silt of sunken city? Or watched the ice fields of Siberia melt into daisy-dotted washing-powder meadows?

PERCHIK. No, I've not!

SAUL. What! Never danced through the dusty kasbahs of In Salah picking mint leaves from your teeth, or observed the powdery course of the Milky Way as the bombs come down like wind-falls onto Norwegian fjords? The blaze of a watery nation going up in flames. Tell me, have you *never* seen the Kalahari Desert lights, baggage?

PERCHIK. No. I told you, I've no' got a passport.

SAUL. Neither have I, I have an aversion to sand, but I am assured they are quite spectacular. I have never been to Scotland either, but I am assured that it is not. How did you get across Hadrian's Channel without a passport? Ferries wouldn't take you without papers, and you can't walk it at low tide any more.

PERCHIK. I swam.

SAUL. You swam?

PERCHIK. From Berwick to Newcastle.

SAUL. You swam from Berwick to Newcastle?

PERCHIK. Aye.

SAUL. You swam. He swam! Thirty-eight miles! That shows some gristle that does, shows some / bloody gristle.

PERCHIK. I should probably be / going.

He stands. SAUL *immediately forces him down again.*

SAUL. I underestimated you, er – what did you say your name was?

PERCHIK. I didn't. S'Perchik. Peter Perchik.

PERCHIK *holds out a hand in introduction.* SAUL *examines it.*

SAUL. Perchik? Not very Scottish, but that can only be a good thing. It will aid your integration into our native culture and value system. My name is Saul Everard but you may call me Mr Saul. More friendly, don't you think you're bleeding on my floor.

PERCHIK. What's that? (*He looks down.*) Oh. Yeah. Sorry 'bout that.

His knuckles are dripping blood. SAUL *silently passes an already bloody tea towel to him, and* PERCHIK *bandages himself.* SAUL *watches with detached interest.*

SAUL. It's a bit fighty out there tonight?

PERCHIK. Ay. A bit. Got lost in the Asian Quarter.

SAUL. The Asian Quarter? The whole city is the Asian Quarter, you dolt. Except for this shop. Do you want a job?

PERCHIK. What?

SAUL. A job. Do you want one? My last boy has just left me in the lurch and your low horizons and negligible intellect suggest you would be quite perfect for the role.

PERCHIK. But no one's hiring. There's nae jobs anywhere.

SAUL. On the contrary, there is one job in the whole of Bradford and you have had the serendipity to trespass right into it. So. What do you say?

PERCHIK. I dunno – what's the work like?

SAUL. Oh, awful.

PERCHIK. But the pay?

SAUL. Very bad. All round it's an excellent situation.

PERCHIK. Right. Well thanks, but no –

SAUL. Is it about the money?

PERCHIK. No, it's not about the / money.

SAUL. Because it's really quite distasteful / to haggle –

PERCHIK. I don't care about the money!

SAUL. Then don't look a gift horse in the mouth, little Perchik! Or it might eventually come to believe you are a sugar cube and *eat you*.

Pause. SAUL *crosses to the shop door and pulls the blind aside.*

Awful lot of coppers about tonight. Awful lot. You can say what you like about them, but they still have a tremendous sense of *pageantry*, don't you think? Tremendous *flair*. For example (I don't know if you read the papers but) it must take a certain amount of brute strength to physically *peel* an Irishman's kneecap off with just your bare hands – and just because he didn't have a passport! I mean, obviously unpleasant for the Irishman. But a real *spectacle*, nonetheless.

PERCHIK *crosses the shop and looks through the blind himself. He looks back at* SAUL.

PERCHIK. Mr Saul? I've bin thinking 'bout your offer.

SAUL. And?

PERCHIK. And I've decided to reconsider.

SAUL. Tremendous! (*He shakes* PERCHIK's *hand.*) You know I was hoping you would!

PERCHIK. Sounds grand. Thank you. You, er, you get a lot of people coming and going?

SAUL *stops pumping* PERCHIK's *hand.*

SAUL. People?

PERCHIK. Customers, ken.

SAUL. Customers, Perchik?

PERCHIK. Buying things?

SAUL. Oh! You mean 'The Wallets'! Not many, no. You couldn't call it many. The market has become awful hostile of late, what with times being not so much lean as anorexic. And of course it's very hard to get hold of good stock now, you know?

PERCHIK. Imagine it is, aye.

SAUL (*deadly serious*). You imagine? But I didn't ask you to imagine.

PERCHIK. Sorry?

SAUL. I didn't ask you to imagine. How hard it is to get hold of good stock, I mean. It wasn't open for debate. It *is* very *hard* for me to get hold of good stock. Understood?

Pause.

PERCHIK. Ye-ah. Right, Mr Saul. Very hard.

SAUL. Good. Good! And now, Perchik, you must tell me: what exactly are you doing in my shop? Naturally, you're on the hoof from someone. The question is, why?

PERCHIK. I'm a painter.

SAUL. Never mind.

PERCHIK. I was painting. On the palace. In London.

SAUL. A-ha. And what, Peter Perchik the Painter, were you painting?

PERCHIK. It was a... portrait. Of sorts.

SAUL. Of sorts?

PERCHIK. You'd mebbe call it an... erotic impression.

SAUL. Of who? The King?

PERCHIK. Nah. Of the PM.

SAUL. Aha. And what was the Prime Minister doing in this erotic impression?

PERCHIK. He wasnay really doing anything. Not that you could see.

SAUL. Not very erotic.

PERCHIK. But you know the Statue of Liberty?

SAUL. Intimately.

PERCHIK. Well, she was sitting on his face.

SAUL. Ha! Excellent. You're going to fit in nicely round here, Perchik, though I don't much care for your methods. Altogether too cerebral. Utopia will be born from the body and not from the mind. When the body is ordered, society follows. Do you see?

PERCHIK. No.

SAUL. Good! Now, my scrofulous whelp, just *one more thing*: do you know what a tinderbox is?

PERCHIK. Yeah – s'for fire-lighting and that.

SAUL. And that. Yes. Well, this shop is a veritable tinderbox. The walls are little more than parchment, and what you must remember is: who holds the matches, little Susan?

PERCHIK. My name's Perchik.

SAUL. I prefer Susan. It suits you better and brings out the blue in your eyes. Who holds the matches, little Susan?

PERCHIK. You do?

SAUL. Very good! Mr Saul holds the matches. You look a bit like a match, you know that? That swollen, scabby skull atop a stick of a body. Best not go rubbing your head on the walls, eh?

PERCHIK. Listen, can I stay here – just for tonight, I mean?

SAUL. No fixed abode, eh? Yes, very well. There's a mattress out back, you can bring it in here. Don't mind the stains. It's only blood. Now. Any questions?

PERCHIK. Ay. As it happens. What happened to your foot?

SAUL. My father fired an airgun at it during our annual family cricket tournament.

PERCHIK. Why?

SAUL. He said it was a joke. He had a funny sense of humour, my dad. Anything else?

PERCHIK. No. I mean yeah. Just one thing. What exactly do you sell?

14

SAUL. Dreams, baggage.

PERCHIK. Wha'?

SAUL. The stuff dreams are made of. That is to say, meat.

He pulls the sheet off the display counter to reveal a pathetic show of sad-looking cuts. He pulls out the pocket watch and examines it.

(*Whispering.*) Now, zip your lip and do as I say. Quiet now.

He unlocks the shop door, then deliberately opens and closes it with a slam. SAUL *gestures to* PERCHIK *to hide behind the counter.* PERCHIK *follows. After a moment,* VANESSA *tentatively pokes her head out of the sack.* SAUL *jumps up.*

Vanessa! You've come out! Marvellous, it's like our honeymoon all over again!

She tries to get to the icebox, jumping as if in a sack race, but SAUL *grabs her.*

You're awful skittish today, my love, all this running about will be no good for your weak ankles. Give me a kiss.

VANESSA *shakes her head. He puts something in her hand.*

Give me a kiss.

She kisses him.

Thank you. And now, Vanessa *this* is a young man from *Scotland*. His name is *Perchik* which is rather ugly but at least it matches his face so we all know *where we stand*.

VANESSA. Hello, Perchik.

PERCHIK. Hello, Vanessa.

SAUL. That's right, that's right, get acquainted. Perchik, *this* is my wife.

VANESSA. I might just have a little smokey…

She reaches to a key hanging on a hook, tied to a long ribbon. The ribbon runs up through the floorboards to upstairs. Next to it is a small wall-mounted cupboard. VANESSA *unlocks the cabinet and takes out a rumpled, nearly empty packet of fags.*

SAUL. Common-law, but then she's a common girl. You've already had two today, wife.

VANESSA. Just to steady my / nerves…

She sticks a fag in her mouth, puts the pack back and locks the cupboard.

SAUL. Common, Perchik, is a politically correct way of saying vulgar. Vulgar is a refined way of saying trampy. Trampy is a slightly more coy word for sluttish. And by slut, Perchik, I mean, of course, that she puts it about, which is in itself an idiom dependent on a shared understanding between interlocutor and receiver of exactly what 'it', the great indefinite of our age, is.

He takes out a long box of matches and lights VANESSA*'s cigarette. As he talks,* SAUL *rummages in the sack* PERCHIK *arrived in, fishes out a few paltry bits of meat, wipes them with his hankie and slaps them straight into the display counter.*

No good if one of you thinks the term refers to apple strudel, now, is it? (Away from the *meat*, wife!) In the eighteenth century, she would have been a whorish orange-seller, you see, but in these days of bad health and halitosis skies, the orange trees spend their days gasping for breath and so she must say it out right. Say it out right, wife.

VANESSA. No –

SAUL. Say it out right.

VANESSA. Shan't.

SAUL. Say it out right or I shall smack your bottom in front of Perchik, and I think he might enjoy the spectacle a little too much.

VANESSA. Leave the boy alone.

SAUL. The boy wants to hear what you have to say, Vanessa. Say it.

VANESSA. No.

SAUL. This is my shop and Empire and while you're within her boundaries you'll do as I say! Or you will be put into jail at His Majesty's Pleasure.

VANESSA. You don't have a jail.

SAUL. Well, then I will put you in a sack. And post you.

PERCHIK. Where?

SAUL. What?

PERCHIK. Where will you post her?

SAUL. I don't know! Somewhere degenerate with an unfavourable exchange rate. (*Beat.*) France. Now say it!

VANESSA. I always thought that was a strange phrase. 'At His Majesty's Pleasure.' Imagine the King grinning at the thought of all the poor souls that he's locked up, away from the sky and the blossom and the stars blanking away in the indigo sky.

SAUL. I won't have poetry in this shop, wife, you know that. *Now say it!*

VANESSA. No.

SAUL. Yes!

VANESSA. NO!

SAUL. *Vanessa...*

Pause.

VANESSA (*quietly*). I'll give you a kiss for a quid.

SAUL. A kiss for a quid! Disgusting! Pity the morally cankered, innocent little Perchik, but mind you don't get too close. Whatever my wife has, it may be infectious.

VANESSA. Do be quiet, Saul.

SAUL. I remember the first kiss we had together, Perchik, it was on the night before the riots started and it tasted distinctly metallic.

VANESSA. Nonsense. Tell him the proper story.

She starts to wheeze.

SAUL. Never kiss a bought woman. All your food will start tasting like pennies.

VANESSA. You're getting me upset. You know it's not good for me. I better sit down.

PERCHIK *brings her a stool but she sits on the floor.*

SAUL. My wife has trouble breathing. Her tubes close up. Her body hates her. I don't hate her. I love her. Together we are waging a war against the enemy body. Watch.

He pushes her into a prone position, sits on her chest and holds her nose. He takes the cigarette from her and blows smoke into her mouth.

Show it who's boss, wife.

PERCHIK. Stop it. Don't do that.

SAUL. What? What was that, contraband? Did you say something?

PERCHIK. Nut. She's going to suffocate, s'all.

SAUL. Not if she knows what's good for her she won't.

VANESSA *is crying and wheezing.*

Show it who's boss, leather lungs! Relax the old pipes! Mind over matter!

She finally pushes him off, and moves onto her hands and knees.

See! Well done, wife, very *well done*!

VANESSA (*choking*). You're a bastard, Saul.

SAUL. On the contrary, Vanessa, unlike you, my mother was a saint and I am one hundred per cent legitimate. Ah, if you'd met Mother Everard, Perchik. She was really something. Put a live crab in her vest every morning to keep her on her toes and always a hot supper on the table. Now that's a woman. Not like Emphysema Annie here.

VANESSA. Could I have some water, please?

SAUL *phlegms into his handkerchief.* PERCHIK *pours her some water from a bottle into a pint glass.*

PERCHIK. You shouldn't smoke. It's bad for you.

VANESSA. Most of the things I love are.

She takes the glass from PERCHIK, *but* SAUL *snatches it away.*

SAUL. Ah-ah-ah! Think before you drink!

He bangs a poster Blu-Tacked to the wall, that reads 'THINK
before you DRINK!' with a sad water droplet under it, then to a
black line drawn around the pint glass like a WWII bathtub. He
pours most of the water back. VANESSA *gulps down what's left.*

We are very careful of water in my Empire, Perchik, because we
know its treachery. Once, we came home to find this very shop
under two feet of the stuff.

VANESSA. When we were still in Barking, this was, Perchik.

SAUL. The arse-end of London proper, flooded so that more salu-
brious postcodes should be saved. Standing where you are now,
we were, water up to our shins.

VANESSA. We began packing up, there and then. Everything we
could take, we took.

SAUL. Took us eight hours to chisel the tiles off the wall.

VANESSA. This counter has travelled over two hundred miles,
Perchik!

SAUL. Put the lot in the van and drove through the night.

VANESSA. And thank goodness we did! Because then –

SAUL. Because then, Perchik, the waters of Barking began to
rise…

VANESSA. The River Roding spilled its banks!

SAUL. Just as the Tiber foamed with blood / before it!

VANESSA. Everything swimming in dirty water, kiddies crying on
/ rooftops –

SAUL. Within three months, all our friends and neighbours were
dead.

PERCHIK. All of them?

SAUL. Well, either dead or very, very *damp*.

PERCHIK. But why here? Why Bradford?

SAUL. You recall, Perchik, that my Empire and I only narrowly
escaped a drowning? And understand we were not anxious to
repeat the experience?

VANESSA. Well, Bradford, you see, Perchik, is unusual for being one of the *only cities in England* to be built away from large bodies of water.

SAUL. See, baggage? (*He taps his head.*) Not just a hatrack!

VANESSA. Also, our petrol ran out, didn't it, Saul?

SAUL. Well, yes. That too.

VANESSA. By the time the drought was over, well, we couldn't face going through the whole palaver again. Saul was having funny turns as it was, weren't you, dear?

SAUL. I am not fond of *change*, Perchik. It disturbs my placid disposition. You'd do well to bear that in mind. Now, as Perchik will be staying with us, Nessa, I'd like you to make the place nice for him. Take your knickers out of the fridge, that sort of thing. Housewifery does not come easily to my wife. She was brought up in the lap of luxury and is unaccustomed to menial tasks such as the wiping of her bottom.

VANESSA. It was hardly luxury, Saul.

SAUL. Compared to what I had, it was. Compared to what I had –

VANESSA. I grew up on a council estate on the Roman Road.

SAUL. Stop trying to spoil the romance of our relationship! I'm your bit of rough! Isn't that exciting, Perchik?

PERCHIK. Do yous have any kids, like?

SAUL. What a question! No. We are not blessed with an heir.

VANESSA. No, but tell him, Saul.

SAUL. Tell him what?

VANESSA. Tell him about Enoch and Maggie.

SAUL. You tell him if you want it told. Come on, Perchik. Time to learn the drill.

He goes to the counter and starts slamming knives onto the surface.

VANESSA. We did have kids, Perchik. Two.

SAUL. All utensils must be thoroughly disinfected.

VANESSA. A boy and a girl.

SAUL. I am scrupulous in my regard for Health and Safety.

He coughs up some more phlegm into his handkerchief.

VANESSA. They died, Perchik.

SAUL. They didn't *die*, Perchik. They were *slaughtered*.

PERCHIK. Slaughtered? By who?

SAUL. By people like you. Immigrants with backpacks and accents. During the 2012 attacks on Stratford. Floor!

He hands PERCHIK *a broom.* PERCHIK *starts to sweep.*

VANESSA. That's how I got this. (*She points to her scar.*) Only went for the day.

SAUL. I warned her. I said to her, I said the whole shebang was just an open invitation to rabid ragheads. What did I say, Vanessa?

VANESSA. You said that the whole shebang was just an open invitation to rabid ragheads.

SAUL. See? Get right into those corners, Perchik!

VANESSA. But they were mad for the ice-dancers, you see. My little munchkins.

SAUL. I wanted to have more but Vanessa has failed us in that way – her uterus is now dryer than a dead camel's tongue. My wife may be a fine actress but even she cannot emote a working reproductive system. (*He hands* PERCHIK *a bin bag.*) Chuck that.

PERCHIK *nervously opens the door. The riots are heard. He chucks the bin bag out.*

PERCHIK. An actress, ay? Will I have seen you in anything?

SAUL. You'll need an apron.

SAUL *crosses to* PERCHIK *with a number of blood-stained white aprons of varying lengths, and tries to find the best fit.*

VANESSA. Oh no. My career never really took off.

SAUL. Don't be so *modest*, wife! Vanessa here was the *star* of a series of short party-political pornographic films intended to broaden the appeal of the Conservative Party to the masses!

VANESSA. Featuring Great Englishmen of History, Perchik. All the big ones they did: Winston Churchill –

SAUL *puts the apron on* PERCHIK *and ties it, standing behind him.*

SAUL. *We Will Fuck Them on the Beaches –*

VANESSA. Francis Drake…

SAUL. *The Spanish Arse-mada –*

VANESSA. It was all proper. Lovely costumes. I played Lady Hamilton wearing silk skirts and a powdered wig.

SAUL. In *Fellatio Nelson.*

PERCHIK *stares at* VANESSA, *wide-eyed.*

PERCHIK (*whispering*). *Fellatio Nelson*?

VANESSA (*solemnly*). It was a bestseller.

SAUL. Yes, Vanessa was worth a good deal of money when I met her.

PERCHIK. How do you know?

SAUL. Because I bought her, didn't I! Bought her out of it!

VANESSA. Saved me.

SAUL. I can't stand to see a woman defiled. It was the same when I was younger and used to run an agency making flats in West London affordable to young Eastern European girls.

PERCHIK. How d'you do that then?

SAUL. By helping them sublet by the hour to businessmen from the Home Counties.

VANESSA. Ever so charitable you are, aren't you, Saul?

SAUL. It's just my character, dearest. Now, what about some supper for Perchik?

VANESSA. Um. There's your stew, Saul…

SAUL. Perfect! A fine introduction to our customs. The way to a country's heart is through its stomach. No, no, wife. *I* shall fetch it!

SAUL *exits with ceremony.*

VANESSA (*fondly*). My husband is a very keen cook.

PERCHIK. Ay? What's his speciality then?

VANESSA. Well... he's very good at brown things. Not like me, I'm shocking, I'd burn a banana split! It comes of not having had a mum for very long I think, there's a certain kind of knowledge that gets passed down isn't there certain things like how to choose a good tomato and pricking sausages with a fork though that said I do make very good pastry, cold hands you see goodness listen to me banging on about myself! I'm sorry, er, Perchik, was it? Saul's right, it is a funny name, isn't it – I don't mean that in a horrible way – so what are you doing in our shop then, Perchik?

PERCHIK (*not missing a beat*). I've come to fix your pianoforte, Lady Hamilton.

As VANESSA spins round sharply, SAUL enters bearing a stockpot and ladle. VANESSA and PERCHIK break gaze as VANESSA rushes out to the back.

SAUL. Ta-da! This'll put some strength in you, Perchik! Are you handy with a spade?

PERCHIK. Dunno. Never used one.

SAUL. You'll soon pick it up. Foundations must be laid!

PERCHIK. Foundations for what?

SAUL. For the extension! I'm expanding my Empire out back.

SAUL tucks his hankie into his shirt-neck. VANESSA enters with bowls and cutlery, and starts laying the table.

And you are going to help me!

PERCHIK. Vanessa and I were just havin' a wee chat about –

VANESSA *quickly holds out a salt-shaker and a pepper-grinder.*

VANESSA. Saul! Condiments to the chef!

SAUL *stares at the salt and pepper for a moment, then they both roar with laughter.*

SAUL. Condiments to the – !

VANESSA (*giggling*). You will be careful, won't you? Out back?

SAUL. Of course we will.

VANESSA. Only, I wouldn't want Perchik to leave like Frankie.

SAUL. Not now, Vanessa.

PERCHIK. What happened to Frankie?

SAUL. Nothing happened to him. Who said anything happened to him?

PERCHIK. I just meant – why did he leave, like? Did he find another position?

SAUL. Yes. He found another position. At a more… grass-roots level.

VANESSA. But, Saul, he didn't –

SAUL. I'm trying not to frighten the boy, Vanessa.

VANESSA. But he should know…

PERCHIK. Know what?

SAUL. It's a sad story. A very sad story.

VANESSA. Oh, ever so sad, Perchik.

PERCHIK. What happened?

SAUL. Oh, I couldn't possibly say. No, it's too sad. I couldn't. No. I'd sooner die. Not even if you begged me on hand and knee I couldn't. Not in a million trillion billion –

PERCHIK. Please?

SAUL. He fell.

VANESSA. Into the cement mixer, Perchik.

SAUL. It was dreadful, I can't deny it, but entirely consonant with the laws of gravity, as I understand them. We were out back. Expanding the Empire. The boy was blind as a bat – he was a foreign as well, like you, no papers, barely spoke a word of English.

VANESSA. Saul is very socially minded.

SAUL. Thank you, wife. I appreciate that.

VANESSA. He's always taking people in, giving them a job.

SAUL. Even in these lean times, an Englishman must behave as an Englishman.

VANESSA. Oh, but so few do.

SAUL. Yes, so few do.

VANESSA. Go to the lengths you go to.

SAUL. I can't say it's not a daily struggle.

VANESSA. I mean, he's not a wealthy man himself.

SAUL. Never aspired to be.

VANESSA. But what he does for these poor foreign blind boys.

SAUL. Just a little education.

VANESSA. And don't they love him for it!

SAUL. They're like sons to me.

VANESSA. Like family.

SAUL. That's enough, wife. One lump or two?

SAUL *starts to dish up stew for himself and* VANESSA. *It is indeed a stew of indistinguishable fleshy lumps (see* Delia Smith's Cookery Course *(1981), p.332).*

VANESSA. Little Francesco. Two please, Saul.

SAUL. Dig in, Perchik.

PERCHIK. I'm. Ah. I'm no' that hungry.

Pause.

SAUL. You're 'no' that hungry'?

VANESSA. But everyone is hungry, Perchik.

PERCHIK. I don't have a very big appetite.

SAUL. Do you know the lengths I go to to put meat on this table? You think it's easy? Essex underwater and Dorset dissolving into the sea like sherbet. There's no pasture any more, no grazing, and here I present you with a delicious stew and you turn up your nose!

VANESSA. Frankie never used to eat much either. The amount of work he did on the food you gave him, Saul. The boy was a real treasure.

PERCHIK. I don't want to seem ungrateful, but –

VANESSA. Actually, Perchik reminds me a bit of Frankie, Saul.

SAUL. If you don't mind me saying, you're being very short-sighted.

VANESSA. Ah, see, Frankie was long-sighted.

SAUL. How long do you think this heat can continue? Only those with enough food stores about their person have any hope of making it through the winter we will have.

PERCHIK. I'm just not –

As SAUL *talks, he lifts out a ladle of stew. Sitting on top is a pair of NHS spectacles.* VANESSA *panics.* SAUL *and* PERCHIK *are oblivious.*

SAUL. We must make ourselves into living larders, that is what we must do, for, to paraphrase the late, great / Charles Darwin –

VANESSA. Um… Saul –

SAUL. 'The human race will soon boil down to little more than survival of the / fattest.'

VANESSA. Saul –

SAUL. And you, you scrawny runt, won't last a minute!

VANESSA. *Saul!*

SAUL *looks from her to the ladle. Sees. Starts. Chucks the ladle back into the pot.*

On the other hand, nobody likes a fatso.

PERCHIK. Aw, go on then, just give us a few tatties. You're right, I should –

SAUL. No, I'm not.

PERCHIK. What?

SAUL. Don't listen to me! I've always had an unhealthy relation-ship with food!

VANESSA. He was chubby as a child!

PERCHIK. Och, now you're offended, I didnay mean – Just think my stomach must've shrunk, that's all, been that long since I ate properly –

SAUL. And how well you look on it! Doesn't he, Vanessa!

VANESSA. Oh yes. Very handsome.

SAUL. What?!

VANESSA. If you like that sort of thing, I mean.

PERCHIK. You're just trying to be polite.

SAUL. How dare you! I'd never dream of it.

PERCHIK. I'll just have a little taste – to show my appreciation, like.

SAUL. No – you mustn't.

PERCHIK. Why not?

SAUL. Because – because… because Vanessa spat in it! Didn't you, wife?

VANESSA. Did I?

SAUL *whacks her with his stick.*

Ow! Oh yeah. I forgot. I'm disgusting, I am. Spit in anything.

SAUL. One of her charming little habits.

VANESSA. Like a bloody llama, me.

PERCHIK *takes the ladle from* SAUL.

PERCHIK. Really, I don't mind. I wouldnay want to insult my hostess.

SAUL *snatches it back.*

SAUL. Ah, but you see, she spends an awful lot of time licking unpalatable objects in public toilets, so I wouldn't dream of asking –

PERCHIK *firmly takes the ladle back.*

PERCHIK. It's fine! I shouldnay've made such a fuss in the first –

PERCHIK *ladles out a spoonful of stew. The glasses are sitting on top. There is a pause as the three of them stare at the object.*

SAUL. The riots are quiet tonight, don't you think?

PERCHIK. Saul? Where did these come from?

SAUL. This blasted heat, I find it very draining. Don't you, Vanessa?

PERCHIK. Are they yours?

VANESSA. Saul has excellent vision.

SAUL. Shut up, wife.

PERCHIK (*to* VANESSA). They're no' yours, are they though?

VANESSA. I should think not.

SAUL. I don't care for what you're insinuating.

PERCHIK. I'm not insinuating nothing.

SAUL. I offer you my pot and you start fishing out bits of old junk.

VANESSA. Calm down, Saul –

SAUL. I will not! There's one thing I can't abide and that's fussy eaters!

PERCHIK. I just wondered what a pair of glasses was doin' in your stew.

SAUL. Waste not want not, Perchik. 'Dig for Victory' etcetera etcetera.

PERCHIK. Whose are they, Saul? Are they – They're not – Jesus.

The penny drops. Beat. VANESSA *suddenly sobs loudly.*

They're Frankie's. Aren't they, Saul? Saul? *Saul?*

SAUL. I did not ask for the Spanish Inquisition, Perchik! (*Beat.*) But seeing as you ask… I thought it a shame that such a… serendipitous bounty should go to waste.

Pause. SAUL *polishes his cutlery intently*. VANESSA *stifles her sobs*.

PERCHIK (*quietly*). How did he get in the cement mixer, Saul?

VANESSA. It was an accident. Wasn't it, Saul! A tragic twist of fate!

PERCHIK. Saul?

SAUL. I told you. He fell.

PERCHIK. Yeah, but *why*? People don't just –

SAUL. We were laying foundations. I stumbled over a spade young Frankie had carelessly left lying on the floor.

PERCHIK. And?

SAUL. And what?! And I may have knocked him with my elbow in my attempts to steady myself! Alright!

Beat.

VANESSA. But – you said that it was an accident. You said he *fell*.

SAUL. He did fall.

VANESSA. But… you pushed him.

SAUL. I… manipulated his centre of gravity, yes. Accidentally.

PERCHIK. And then he fell.

SAUL. I can't be held responsible for his trajectory thereafter.

VANESSA. But you pushed him.

SAUL. Don't be so naïve, Vanessa. He had a terrible life. Terrible.

VANESSA. He was happy here, Saul.

SAUL. Worked his arse off –

VANESSA. We used to sing together –

SAUL. And for what? For a pittance! And you remember that disgusting acne –

VANESSA. It was characterful.

SAUL. It was pus-ful. His life was a waste of harvestable organs.

VANESSA. But you told me he fell.

.. I was trying to spare your feelings. It wasn't my fault.

CHIK. But you pushed him.

VANESSA. He loved it here.

SAUL. Course he did.

VANESSA. Called me 'Mamma Vanessa'.

SAUL. Better than the godforsaken rathole he came from.

PERCHIK begins to edge away from the table.

VANESSA. Fitted in well.

SAUL. Forty degrees in the shade and women with hairy armpits.

VANESSA. Like it was his home.

SAUL. WELL, IT WASN'T HIS HOME, WAS IT!

Still looking at VANESSA, SAUL stabs his fork into PERCHIK's leg and holds it there. PERCHIK yelps then writhes in silent agony. VANESSA weeps quietly.

VANESSA. I thought… I thought it was an accident… Poor Frankie…

SAUL (*conversationally*). My wife has a very sensitive disposition. As a young girl she used to cry at compost heaps.

VANESSA. I did not. Last time I cried was when me mum died.

SAUL. You're awful talkative tonight, wife. Come here.

He lets go of the fork, grabs VANESSA's wrist and pulls her onto his lap. PERCHIK pulls the fork out of his leg with relief, and breathes deeply.

I think the pair of you are forgetting who holds the matches here. Discipline, Perchik, is the cornerstone of any Empire. I find the old methods remain the best, over time.

He turns VANESSA over on his knee, pulls up her skirt and pulls down her knickers.

VANESSA. Saul!

SAUL. Now, Perchik, give it a smack, she won't feel it, it's like donkey hide. The whole region is like donkey hide. The meaning of that simile is that my wife's nether regions have no sensation. The result of years of overuse, eh, my flower?

He smacks her, hard. She struggles, trying to cover herself.

VANESSA. Ow! Saul, stop it, not in front / of him, please – Saul!

SAUL. Have a go. It's great fun.

PERCHIK. No, thanks all the same.

SAUL. No?

PERCHIK. ... Nah. You're alright.

SAUL. Do you have any testicles, Perchik? Or do you just view them as useful if inconveniently located paperweights?

PERCHIK. I jus' don't think it's – appropriate.

SAUL. Nonsense! Come over and give her a smack now! Plant it right *there*.

He smacks her again to indicate the spot. PERCHIK *crosses to them. He stands for a moment, raises his hand, then leans over and softly kisses* VANESSA's *bottom.*

Eh? What's all this? Who said you could kiss my wife's arse?

PERCHIK. You did.

SAUL. I did not!

PERCHIK. I must have misunderstood. You should give your invitations more clarity in future.

SAUL (*disbelieving*). I should what? You little –

PERCHIK. A slip of the tongue, a flawed e-nun-cia-tion. Can send the whole meaning of your sentence into chaos.

SAUL. You... you... get in the van. We're going for a drive.

Beat. SAUL *throws* VANESSA *off his lap and grabs* PERCHIK.

PERCHIK. Ay? Where we going?

SAUL. Calais.

PERCHIK. I don't want to go to Calais.

SAUL. No one *wants* to go to Calais. Even people who *live* in Calais don't *want* to go to Calais. It's a stinking grey mudbank reeking of pilchards. It would be like wanting to wear a syphilitic streetwalker's knickers as a sunhat. But nonetheless, we're going.

VANESSA. Don't hurt him, Saul, he didn't mean anything by it.

SAUL. Who said anything about hurting him? I didn't.

VANESSA. But you said you were taking him / to Calais.

SAUL. Yes. Calais was mentioned, hurting him was not. Vanessa's confused, Perchik, perhaps my enunciation was flawed.

PERCHIK. Perhaps it was.

SAUL. Are you trying to be clever?

PERCHIK. No. Not trying.

SAUL. You ungrateful little – !

Suddenly there's a banging at the door. All three start.

DETECTIVE PRAWN (*off*). This is Detective Prawn. Open up!

VANESSA. They know, Saul! About Frankie! Oh God! I can't – I / can't breathe!

SAUL. Don't get hysterical, wife.

DETECTIVE PRAWN (*off*). I can hear you in there!

SAUL (*panicking*). Just coming, Detective! Get the door, Perchik. Quickly!

PERCHIK. You've got to be kidding?

SAUL. Oh yes! I look like I'm in a puckish mood, do I?

PERCHIK. What I meant was, if I do, that they'll come in here and – you know.

SAUL. Of course they won't.

PERCHIK. Oh no? And what makes you think that?

SAUL. Because I won't tell them who you are, you fetid little arse-kisser! Now get the blasted door before I decide to introduce you as Colin the paedo cop-killer!

PERCHIK *flings open the door. As he does,* VANESSA *notices Frankie's glasses.*

VANESSA. The spectacles, Saul!

SAUL *panics, then puts the spectacles on. Gravy drips down his face.* DETECTIVE PRAWN *enters.*

DETECTIVE PRAWN. Who's in charge of this establishment?

SAUL. Hello. This is my shop. This is my wife. And this is... Um...

VANESSA. *Francesco.* Frankie.

SAUL. Yes! Very good, wife. This is Frankie, my – Frankie. He's Italian.

PERCHIK *throws a panicked look at* SAUL, *then smiles.*

PERCHIK. Er... Ciao, bella!

DETECTIVE PRAWN. I've not got time for 'Ciao, bellas'! A dangerous painter is on the loose!

SAUL. The worst kind! Perhaps we can help. What does he look like?

DETECTIVE PRAWN. He looks... like a painter.

VANESSA. Which one?

DETECTIVE PRAWN. All of them.

VANESSA. All of them?

DETECTIVE PRAWN. What I mean to say is that he has a generic artistic *countenance*. (*Beat.*) You know. Shifty.

VANESSA. But why would you think he's here?

DETECTIVE PRAWN. We have intelligence to suggest that he hitched a lift from London and arrived at a landfill site here in Bradford at around four-thirty this afternoon.

VANESSA. How do you know it was him?

DETECTIVE PRAWN. The car that he flagged down was an unmarked police car driven by my Superior, DCI Swann. It seems this 'artist' is an exceptionally stupid character.

VANESSA. But why didn't DCI Swann arrest him?

DETECTIVE PRAWN. He's not too bright either.

SAUL. I'm sorry, Detective. We've not seen anyone of that description, but of course we'll let you know if… What?

>*SAUL stops. DETECTIVE PRAWN is staring at him.*

DETECTIVE PRAWN. Umm… there's gravy on your face, sir.

SAUL. Sorry?

DETECTIVE PRAWN. There's gravy.

SAUL. Where?

DETECTIVE PRAWN. On your face.

SAUL. Oh.

>*Beat.*

DETECTIVE PRAWN. Why is there gravy on your face, sir?

SAUL. Why is there gravy on my face? Why is there gravy on my… What an *excellent* question, the reason is – The reason, I mean to say –

PERCHIK. It's our custom, Officer.

DETECTIVE PRAWN. What?

PERCHIK. Er – I mean… it'sa oura customa! Ciao, bella!

SAUL. Yes! Very good, P… Frankie! Our custom! A silly little custom of ours. If we've had an exceptionally good meal, to, ah – show our appreciation we put – um –

DETECTIVE PRAWN. Gravy on your face, sir?

SAUL. Exactly!

DETECTIVE PRAWN. I see. You must waste a lot of gravy.

SAUL. Not really. My wife is a very mediocre cook.

DETECTIVE PRAWN. I'm sorry. You, er – You mind if I have a taste?

>*He picks up the ladle,* VANESSA *swipes it off him.*

VANESSA. Won't you spoil your dinner, Detective?

DETECTIVE PRAWN. Oh no. Mrs Prawn has recently become a freegan.

VANESSA. A freegan?

DETECTIVE PRAWN. She'll only eat food out of skips. Ecologically it's very sound, but I can't say it's not damaged our standing on Bradford's dinner-party circuit. You mind?

He takes the ladle from VANESSA *and ladles out some stew.*

SAUL. No!

VANESSA. No!

PERCHIK. No... -a!

Sitting on top of the ladle is a flip-flop.

DETECTIVE PRAWN (*staring down*). *What the hell is this?*

SAUL. It was an accident!

VANESSA. He fell!

Silently, SAUL *takes a cricket bat from behind the counter, creeps behind* DETECTIVE PRAWN *and raises it. But* DETECTIVE PRAWN *isn't looking at the flip-flop. He produces a pair of tweezers, then lifts something from the floor. It's a cigarette butt. He rises with a nasty grin.* SAUL *chucks the cricket bat behind him.*

DETECTIVE PRAWN. Oh-ho-ho. You are *for it*, mate.

SAUL. Is there a problem, Detective?

DETECTIVE PRAWN. Tell me – is this your shop?

SAUL. Yes. It's my shop. And Empire, Detective.

DETECTIVE PRAWN. And so, sir, does this – *cigarette butt* belong to you?

SAUL. No. I've never seen it before in my life. But if I had to make a guess, I'd say it belonged to the unruly gang of sado-masochistic asthmatics who use my property for their 'Wine, Wheeze and Cheese Evenings', every last Sunday of the month.

DETECTIVE PRAWN. Don't try and be *funny*, fella. Tobacco and its derivatives are designated a Class-A drug, and the purchase and consumption of their associated products is a serious offence. You're looking at five to ten in a prison full of Estonian gangsters and kiddy-fiddlers with dubious personal hygiene and I've heard bathtime can get a bit friendly, so why don't you just ANSWER THE FUCKING QUESTION!

Pause. PERCHIK *picks up the cricket bat. Then suddenly* DETECTIVE PRAWN *grins.*

Aaahhh! Only kidding! I've got six rapes and an identity theft to write up tonight! Last thing I want is fourteen hours of paper-work over this! But I got you, didn't I!

He starts to wander again, poking his head round doors, then approaches the icebox.

SAUL. Oh yes, Detective! Yes! You got me!

All three relax and laugh matily along.

DETECTIVE PRAWN. The look on your face! Priceless! Well, you've got to laugh, haven't you? What have we got here? (*He opens the icebox door, looks in.*) What I'm always saying to my colleagues, in a job like ours, you really have got to laugh...

SAUL. Oh yes, Detective! You've got to laugh!

DETECTIVE PRAWN. Otherwise you'll... (*He turns suddenly.*) Hang on. Was that – a *flip-flop*?

Quick as a flash, PERCHIK *chucks the cricket bat to* SAUL, *who brings it down on* DETECTIVE PRAWN's *head. He collapses into the icebox.*

PERCHIK. Here.

PERCHIK *helps* SAUL *manoeuvre* DETECTIVE PRAWN *into the sack that* PERCHIK *arrived in.* VANESSA *opens the shop door and peers out.*

VANESSA. Quick! There's a lorry backing up!

SAUL *and* PERCHIK *carry the sack out of the door. The sound of an engine starting up is heard as they re-enter, exhausted.* VANESSA *collapses with relief.*

Well! I think that could have gone a lot worse. Don't you?

SAUL *chucks the spectacles in the pot, then marches on*
PERCHIK. *He's spoiling to lamp him. At the last moment,*
SAUL *takes out his hankie and phlegms into it.*

SAUL. Nicely done, baggage.

PERCHIK. Thanks. Listen, sorry about before. I shouldn't / have –

SAUL. Vanessa?

VANESSA. Yes, Saul?

SAUL. Tell Perchik the next time he considers kissing my wife's
bottom, he should remember which one of us has papers and
which one does not.

SAUL *exits.* VANESSA *turns to* PERCHIK.

VANESSA. My husband said to tell you the next time you
consider –

PERCHIK. I heard.

VANESSA *pulls out her workbox. She sits and starts to sew.*
PERCHIK *watches her intently. The muffled sound of 'Pomp
and Circumstance' starts up above them.*

VANESSA. I'm glad you came, Perchik. I think we're going to be
good good friends. Only, you must try not to upset Saul. He's an
old man, you see. He's a bit stuck in his ways but that's only
natural can you stop staring at me please?

PERCHIK (*embarrassed*). Sorry. I just… Sorry. (*Beat.*) What's he
doing up there?

VANESSA. Oh, you know. Blueprints. For the revolution.

PERCHIK. For the revolution. Right. If you don't mind me saying,
your husband – he's a little bit… (*He taps his head.*) Isn't he?
What's it, senile dementia?

VANESSA. No, it's bloody not! He's just… past his prime. Knows
a lot of stuff though.

PERCHIK. About bloody what? Lamb chops and mince?

VANESSA. No. Like, history. Culture and that. He gives me
classes. You'll probably have to do them too. Frankie did. And
Klaus. Only, they never understood much.

'Pomp and Circumstance' gets louder.

PERCHIK. Can't stand that racket. Can't we put something else on?

VANESSA. Don't have nothing, do I? Used to. Used to have loads. Tammy Wynette. She was my favourite. And Edith Piaf. I loved them two. Had all the albums. But they got lost during the move. I swear I put them in at Barking... but when we got here... they were gone. Saul says they must've fallen out of the van. Or been stolen by Gypsy DJs. Or something. I miss my records. Don't get nothing but bloody Elgar now. Hold these.

She hands PERCHIK *a pair of shears to hold as she rummages in her workbox.*

PERCHIK. What you making?

VANESSA. Just some curtains. For the cottage.

PERCHIK. The cottage?

VANESSA takes a scrap of paper out, gives it to PERCHIK, *and continues sewing.*

VANESSA. S'in the country somewhere. By the sea. I forget where. Up north though. More north than Bradford, I mean. Where it still snows. This is just – what d'you call it – *an artist's impression.* S'not finished yet, see. We're building it slowly. 'Brick by bastard brick,' Saul says. (*Confidentially.*) It's got a room *just for boots*, Perchik!

PERCHIK. It's nice, in'it? Pretty.

VANESSA beams at him. She looks beautiful.

VANESSA. It's our dream house! We've waited ten years but it won't be long now. S'taking longer than expected. What with business being so bad. But things'll pick up soon. You could come with us, Perchik! I'm going to paddle in the sea every – ow!

PERCHIK. Are you okay?

VANESSA. Yeah. Just pricked myself.

PERCHIK. Let's see.

VANESSA holds her finger out.

It's bleeding.

VANESSA. Only a bit.

PERCHIK *puts her finger in his mouth and sucks the blood from it.*

What are you –

PERCHIK. You're a very beautiful woman.

VANESSA. What?

PERCHIK. I said. You're a Very. Beautiful. Woman.

Pause. They stare at each other. Then:

VANESSA. Shut up.

PERCHIK. I've always thought so.

VANESSA. Don't be daft, we've only just met.

PERCHIK. I knew it was you. They say the camera adds ten pounds, but I could spot you a mile off.

VANESSA. You mean – before. When you said. I mean… You've seen *Fellatio Nelson*?

PERCHIK. Seen it?! You made me cum like a train twice a day for five years!

VANESSA. You're just saying that.

PERCHIK. No, I'm not! Used to steal me da's mags and films from under his bed, didn't I? Stacks of 'em, he had.

VANESSA. Including those made by the Conservative Party?

PERCHIK. 'Specially those made by the Conservative Party.

VANESSA. I should've thought your father was a Labour man.

PERCHIK. He was blue-curious.

VANESSA. I've never met a fan before.

PERCHIK. You look just the same.

VANESSA. Apart from Saul of course.

PERCHIK. Just as beautiful, / I mean it.

VANESSA. Imagine you sat there / at home.

PERCHIK. Watching you / on the telly.

VANESSA. Watching me / in my powdered wig.

PERCHIK. I can remember it off by heart.

VANESSA. Really?

> PERCHIK *puts one hand inside his shirt, then gallops up to her.*

PERCHIK (*porn voice*). 'Hello, Lady Hamilton. I've come to fix your pianoforte.'

VANESSA. Oh no, Perchik. I can't!

PERCHIK. Aw, go on!

VANESSA. I mean, I shouldn't. That's all in the past, that's – I mean… no.

PERCHIK. Alright then. Suit yeself.

> PERCHIK *shrugs and walks to the blind. Looks through.*
> VANESSA *bites her lip.*

VANESSA. Well. I suppose it wouldn't –

PERCHIK (*quickly*). Yes?

VANESSA. If it was just –

PERCHIK. Of course –

VANESSA. And no one has to –

PERCHIK. No!

VANESSA. What was that you said?

PERCHIK. About your pianoforte?

VANESSA. Yes.

PERCHIK (*grins*). I've come to fix it!

VANESSA. 'Oh Lord Nelson! You've caught me tinkling my ivories in my scanties! How shameful!'

PERCHIK. 'Your scanties are divine, Lady Hamilton. Now that I've seen them, I must have you now, here in this very drawing room!'

VANESSA. 'It's not a drawing room, it's a library.'

PERCHIK. 'Nonetheless!'

VANESSA. 'Oh, but I can't! I mustn't! I won't!'

PERCHIK. 'But England expects that you do, Emma!'

VANESSA. 'Then in the name of England and her outlying lands, I demand that you jizz on my tits, Lord Nelson!'

PERCHIK *seizes* VANESSA *and leans her over his knee.*

PERCHIK. 'Lady Hamilton! I declare you are a pedigree saucepot!'

PERCHIK *suddenly kisses her.* VANESSA *slaps his face. She runs into the icebox.*

Vanessa...

VANESSA (*indistinct through the door and tears*). I'm a married woman, Perchik.

PERCHIK. What?

VANESSA *opens the door. It's quite an operation.*

VANESSA. I said, I'm a married woman!

VANESSA *slams the door again.*

PERCHIK. I'm sorry, Vanessa. Vanessa?

VANESSA (*singing, off*). Oh, the toe bone's connected to the –

PERCHIK. Vanessa. Open the door.

VANESSA (*off*). – *foot* bone, the foot bone's connected to the –

PERCHIK. OPEN THE DOOR!

VANESSA (*off*). – *ankle* bone, the ankle bone's connected to the knee bone...

PERCHIK *sighs and sits. He takes a banana out of his bag.* VANESSA *continues to sing.* SAUL *enters, and makes an OTT show of searching the shop for something.*

SAUL. Where are they then?

PERCHIK (*nervously*). Who? There's nobody here but me, Mr Saul.

SAUL. Oooh! I'm sorry! I'm so – It's just, I assumed from the noise that someone was *trapping cats* down here! (*His smile vanishes.*) If you don't mind I'm trying to – WHAT THE HELL IS THAT?

He gestures at PERCHIK's *banana.*

PERCHIK. It's a banana.

SAUL. I won't have fruit in the shop.

PERCHIK. What the – Why not?

SAUL. It upsets the meat.

PERCHIK. That sausage looks perfectly happy to me.

SAUL. Well, it's crying on the inside. Do you know how many *Phoneutria Fera*, or Brazilian wandering spiders, enter this country illegally in banana crates? By thinking only of your own potassium levels, you are throwing our national ecology into turmoil.

PERCHIK. Potassium levels?

SAUL. I mean, if you *must* indulge the appendix, there are plenty of good *English* fruits you might try. The Cox's orange pippin! The Victoria plum! All fine varieties. But a *banana*, Perchik. A banana? Of all things.

PERCHIK. It's just a banana.

SAUL. It was just cake to Marie Antoinette, my friend.

VANESSA (*off*). NOW HEAR THE WORD OF THE LORD!

SAUL (*irritably*). Shut up, wife!

SAUL *slams his stick against the icebox. The door opens and* VANESSA *creeps out.*

(*Beaming at her.*) Ah! Hello, piglet. Hiding in the icebox again?

VANESSA (*irritably*). Had to cool down, didn't I? Can't stand this bloody heat. Makes my fingers itch.

VANESSA *starts to sew.* PERCHIK *watches.* SAUL *pulls his face round by the chin.*

SAUL. Oi. Goggle-eyes. I don't love her for her brains and she's not much to look at but she's mine and if you touch her I'll feed you your own kidneys.

PERCHIK *laughs nervously.*

What are you laughing at?

PERCHIK. I'm not sure.

SAUL *starts to exit, then turns back and surveys* PERCHIK.

SAUL. I mean. A *banana*.

End of Act One.

ACT TWO

'At the Meat of Things'

We discover SAUL *busy with some paper and glue.* PERCHIK *is leant over a ledger and a calculator at the counter. He taps his pencil. Sighs. Looks up.*

PERCHIK. Mr Saul? These accounts – they're no' very / healthy.

SAUL. Ah-ah-ah!

SAUL *points to what he's doing and puts his finger to his lips.*

PERCHIK. I'm not joking. They're in a really bad way.

SAUL. Yes yes, *later*, Perchik. First: I've made you a present. (*He holds it up.*) A passport, Perchik! To identify you as a citizen of my Empire.

PERCHIK. Oh. Well. Ta.

He goes to take it from SAUL*'s hand, but* SAUL *snatches it back.*

SAUL. No, no, not yet. You haven't *earned* it yet.

PERCHIK. But –

SAUL *holds up a hand: 'quiet'.* PERCHIK *wanders, bored.*

It's hot, ay? I'm hot. Where's everybody? Where's all the customers?

SAUL. Making the most of a blazing February afternoon, I imagine. To some, the melanoma is infinitely fascinating. They may as well enjoy it while it lasts.

PERCHIK. You mean, for ever?

SAUL *snorts in laughter.*

Wha'? You mean you don't believe in climate change?

SAUL. I've told you, I don't believe in *any kind of change at all*.

PERCHIK. Aw, but come on, Mr Saul – what about the heat? The floods!

SAUL. Nothing but an excuse for the English to carry on doing what they love best.

PERCHIK. And what's that then?

SAUL. Talking about the weather.

PERCHIK *wanders to the door and looks through the blind.*

PERCHIK. Come on! Someone! Someone come in!

SAUL. Don't hold your / breath.

PERCHIK. Wait, wait! There's someone coming. Yes! He's definitely… he's at the door.

He runs behind the counter. Long pause. A solitary letter slips through the letterbox.

The postman. It was just the postman.

Deflated, PERCHIK *goes to pick the letter up.*

SAUL. DON'T TOUCH IT!

PERCHIK. S'just a letter.

SAUL *rushes over and pulls* PERCHIK *away.*

SAUL. Don't be so *naïve.* We live in an age of biological warfare. This *letter* could be dripping in anthrax. Or truth drugs!

PERCHIK. And is it?

SAUL *gingerly picks up the envelope and sniffs it.*

SAUL. … No.

PERCHIK *tuts and goes back to the blind.* SAUL *opens the letter.*

PERCHIK (*under his breath*). Who knew the end ay the world would be this fuckin' borin'.

SAUL. Aha!

PERCHIK. Well? Who's it from?

SAUL. Apparently I may have won a substantial cash prize.

PERCHIK *looks back through the blind.*

PERCHIK. We've not had a customer all morning. Not one.

SAUL. Business as usual.

PERCHIK. Why don't you *do* something? You can't survive like this.

SAUL. I have fingers in many pies, Perchik. Only one of them is meat.

PERCHIK. Your fingers or the pies?

Beat.

SAUL. Both.

PERCHIK. Yeah, well, maybe if you worked on your customer service –

SAUL. And what would you know about my customer service?

PERCHIK. I know by looking at the state of these books!

SAUL. Don't you cheek me, ragamuffin! I treat every customer that walks through that door like I would a minor Royal!

WINSTON *enters. He's a flustered English gentleman. He wears a suit similar to* SAUL*'s.*

What the hell do you want?

WINSTON. H-h-h-hullo. I was wondering if you had a spot of h-h-him?

SAUL. Him?

WINSTON. Yes. H-h-h-him. You know. (*Beat.*) As in 'him sandwiches'.

SAUL. Ohhhh! 'Aaaam! Sorry, no pig today. Goodbye.

WINSTON *starts to exit.* PERCHIK *rushes to block the doorway.*

PERCHIK. How about a lovely sausage, sir? I'll bet a man of your impeccable tastes would appreciate a good sausage, sir?

WINSTON. Well, that's very kind of you, but I don't think my tastes are especially –

PERCHIK. Oh, but look at your suit, sir! Look at the gentleman's suit, Mr Saul!

PERCHIK *violently nudges* SAUL *with his elbow and waves the ledger at him.*

WINSTON. This old thing? Do you like it, do you? It was my father's, h-h-h-actually. Terribly old now, I'm afraid. Practically an / antique.

SAUL. Not at all, sir! I admire a man who wears his inheritance on his back! Little hot spell like this is no excuse not to make an *effort*. My dad never went out with a bare head or an empty buttonhole. Immaculate, he was. Compare him to Perchik. Looks like a washing machine vomited, don't he? Do you remember, sir? / The old days?

WINSTON (*chuckles*). Oh yes –

SAUL. When the summers went by in a golden haze –

WINSTON. Gorgeous summers –

SAUL. We never had it so good, did we, sir?

WINSTON. H-h-h-halcyon days.

SAUL. When you could leave your car keys in the ignition and your front door on the latch!

WINSTON. Well h-h-h-actually that's a bit / before my –

SAUL. Or take a girl to the pictures and get change for a thrup-penny bit?

WINSTON. I really don't remember / that far...

SAUL. Cockles from the fishman's barrow on a Sunday night and Gracie Fields singing 'The Largest Aspidistra in the World' on the wireless –

WINSTON. I'm only forty-two!

An icy pause.

SAUL. Alright, sir. No need to get testy. I was only speaking *figuratively*.

WINSTON. I'm sorry, I didn't mean... Oh dear me, how embar-rassing. You must excuse me, I'm just – I'm a little *fraught*. The thing is, I'm terribly worried about my sister.

PERCHIK. Your sister, sir?

WINSTON. We've just arrived in town, you see. And since we left the old pile of bricks –

PERCHIK. Old pile of bricks, sir?

WINSTON. Oh, er – Bootlebum Hall. In Gloucestershire.

PERCHIK. Bootlebum Hall, sir?

WINSTON. Yes.

PERCHIK. In Gloucestershire, sir?

WINSTON. Yes! Do you know it?

PERCHIK. No. Nice place, was it?

WINSTON. Oh yes. It broke poor Constance's heart to leave, but after we had to have the gamekeeper put down, well – there really wasn't h-h-any other option. Connie's been an absolute brick about it, only, since we arrived in Bradford, she's been...well, she's not been tickety-boo.

PERCHIK. Not tickety-boo, sir?

WINSTON. Not tickety-boo at *all*. Pale. Won't eat a scrap, though she says she might manage a little h-h-him, if it was very thinly sliced. I can't think what's caused it.

SAUL. Mark my words, it'll be the water, sir, did you boil it before you drank?

WINSTON. Boil it? Of course we didn't boil it, this isn't *Africa* for goodness' sakes!

SAUL. Ah.

WINSTON. You mean... you think it's – some sort of stomach bug? Delhi belly?

SAUL. I'd say so, sir. Something like that. A stomach bug. Delhi belly. Cholera.

WINSTON. Cholera!

SAUL. I don't mean to upset you, sir, that's merely a worst-case scenario.

PERCHIK. Probably just needs feeding up a wee bit. How about a nice sausage?

WINSTON. Well, that sounds –

SAUL. Put a bit of colour in her cheeks, will a nice sausage. Made fresh this month.

WINSTON. Pork or beef?

SAUL. Hard to say.

PERCHIK whisks a sad little bird body from the counter.

PERCHIK. Or what about this pigeon, sir?

SAUL. Oh, now you cannot underestimate the palliative power of a pigeon, sir!

WINSTON. What are those black marks?

SAUL. Don't worry about that! That's only tyre tracks, that'll come out in the cooking!

WINSTON. I'm not sure… I can't / risk –

WINSTON starts to exit. SAUL shrugs. Quickly, PERCHIK calls after him.

PERCHIK. Is she very pale, sir?

WINSTON turns back, worried.

WINSTON. I, er – Rather pale, yes. Except for a sort of… green tinge.

PERCHIK. Only, sounds like she's got what my poor sausage-starved Auntie Bernice had.

WINSTON. Really?

PERCHIK. Started off pale, she did, couldnay keep nuthin' down. Kept asking for 'him'. Then came the green tinge. Then the bloating.

WINSTON. The bloating?

PERCHIK. Ay. Round like a melon she was. Then the next day, she exploded.

Beat.

WINSTON. Exploded?

PERCHIK. Ay. Exploded. All over ma father's collection of pornographic films.

WINSTON. But… that's terrible.

PERCHIK. I know. Some of them were collector's items.

SAUL. And all for the want of a bit of protein, sir…

WINSTON. I see. Well. In that case. I'd better take the lot.

PERCHIK. *Very* good, sir!

> PERCHIK *starts chucking all the meat into a plastic bag.*

SAUL (*whispering to* PERCHIK). Not the chop.

PERCHIK. Wha'?

SAUL. That chop came all the way from Barking with me. I even gave her a name.

WINSTON. Would you mind awfully h-h-hurrying up?

PERCHIK. Hold your horses, sir. There's still the question of payment.

WINSTON. How much does it cost?

PERCHIK. Well, how much have you got?

WINSTON. Um… fifty?

> SAUL *and* PERCHIK *suck in their breath.*

PERCHIK. Sterling is that, sir? Cannay do nuthin' with sterling. What about your suit, sir?

WINSTON. My suit?

PERCHIK. It's a nice suit. Call it fifty sterling and the suit. Cannay say fairer than that.

WINSTON. Well, I…

PERCHIK. *Kaboom!*

> PERCHIK *does a slow-motion mime of Auntie Bernice exploding.* WINSTON *hurriedly takes off his suit, and swaps it with* SAUL *for the meat.*

WINSTON. The money's h-in the h-inside pocket. Thanks very much.

He rushes out, clutching the meat. SAUL *calls after him.*

SAUL. Not at all, sir! A pleasure to serve you!

The door slams.

Toffee-nosed git.

He turns and stares at PERCHIK.

PERCHIK. What?

SAUL. She *exploded*?

PERCHIK. I was improvising, wasn't I! And it worked, didn't it?

SAUL. Oh *yes*, it worked alright. And now muggins here has to spend the rest of the day restocking! In the meantime, what have we got left to sell? Bugger all!

PERCHIK. There's that lamb chop for a start.

SAUL. You leave Danielle out of this! I've told you how hard it is for me to get good stock! Could be days before we get another delivery!

JOHN *enters.*

JOHN. Delivery!

PERCHIK. Ha! – Ow!

SAUL *has smacked him round the head.*

JOHN. Good morning, Mr Everard!

SAUL. Good morning, John! (*He looks for a sack.*) Where is it then?

JOHN. Oh, for Christ's – (*He calls off.*) JOHN JUNIOR! You great lump of –

JOHN JUNIOR *enters, lugging a sack. He dumps it centre stage.*

SAUL. And what do we have here?

JOHN. You're in luck today, Mr Everard! Articulated lorry hit a Gypsy caravan on the outskirts of Ilkley Moor! Sign here please.

JOHN JUNIOR *pulls a saddle out of the top of the sack and holds it up.*

JOHN JUNIOR. Will you be wanting to keep this, Mr Everard?

SAUL (*signing*). Just leave it out back with the others, John Junior.

JOHN JUNIOR *exits to the back, with the saddle. Suddenly, SAUL, JOHN and PERCHIK are hit with a foul stench.*

JOHN. Listen, you might want t'shift it quick, like. It's, er, on the turn a bit.

SAUL. 'On the turn a bit'!

JOHN. It's this bloody heat. Encourages the growth of bacteria.

SAUL. I paid in advance! I want my money back.

JOHN. I'm sorry, Mr Everard, my hands are tied. You'll have to take it up with the boss.

SAUL. At least take this filth away!

JOHN. Oh no no no, Mr Everard.

JOHN *scribbles on some documents on his clipboard.*

SAUL. What do you mean, 'no no no'? This is fetid. It's crawling with maggots!

JOHN. More than my job's worth, Mr Everard. And where would I put it?

SAUL. Oh, I don't know, John, up your capacious rectum perhaps?

Beat. JOHN *looks up at* SAUL, *who smiles at him.* JOHN JUNIOR *enters from out back.*

JOHN. What?

SAUL. What? (*Beat.*) How's the little one, John?

JOHN JUNIOR. Not so little, Mr Saul!

JOHN JUNIOR *gestures the size of a leviathan baby.*

JOHN. Shut up, lad. (*Beat.*) He's fine, Mr Saul. Baby's fine. (*Beat.*) Listen, I'll tell you what I'll do. JJ? Run back to Mr Womble and express Mr Everard's dissatisfaction. Mr Everard is a loyal and valued customer. He deserves better.

SAUL. Well, thank you, John! I appreciate that.

JOHN. Come on then, lad! Mush! Mush! Mush!

JOHN JUNIOR starts and scampers from the shop.

PERCHIK. Your boss will replace it, will he? The meat?

SAUL. Don't pester the man, Perchik.

PERCHIK. But what will we do? Look at these books, the accounts are a *joke* –

SAUL. Profit and loss, Perchik, profit and loss. The Empire must absorb. And find ways to balance both.

JOHN. I'll be off then.

SAUL. Would you care to inspect our expansion out back, John?

JOHN. I'm a bit pushed for time, to be honest.

SAUL. It really has come on a long way. The foundations are all but completed.

JOHN. Really, I better be –

SAUL. I think you'll be especially impressed with the ground beams…

Beat. PERCHIK *is staring at* SAUL, SAUL *at* JOHN.

JOHN. Yeah. Alright then. Why not, eh? That'd be grand.

SAUL. Excellent! Perchik, run along and make John a nice cup of tea.

PERCHIK. Wha'?

SAUL (*elaborately miming*). MAKE. JOHN. A. CUP. OF. TEA.

PERCHIK. Right. Yeah.

PERCHIK *exits.*

SAUL. You'll have to excuse Perchik, John. He's Scottish. Shall we?

JOHN. Been thinking of building a patio myself. Bit of a suntrap. Get myself a tan.

SAUL. Mmm. Crackling.

JOHN. What?

SAUL. Nothing, nothing. Step this way, John. Only, watch out for the cement mixer. It's a little… precarious.

SAUL and JOHN exit to back. VANESSA enters by the front door, pushing a pram.

VANESSA. Shop! (*Beat.*) *Sho-op!*

No reply. VANESSA shrugs, then produces a cardboard box with 'Cottage' written on it. She pulls item after item out of the pram into the box; twee decorative things – windchimes, china figurines, etc. Finally, she looks round, then brings out a banana. She unpeels it. PERCHIK arrives in the doorway in time to watch as she crams it into her mouth. Lovely. He smiles. Then he hears SAUL approaching. He disappears as SAUL enters, breathless, with a builder's bucket, which he sets down by the doorway.

SAUL. Ah, wife, you're home. Good.

VANESSA hurriedly swallows and holds up a novelty teapot to distract SAUL.

VANESSA. Look! For the cottage, Saul! Amazing, ain't it? It's a *teapot*. But it's shaped *like a cat*!

SAUL. Good God! And yet they still haven't found a cure for cancer!

PERCHIK enters at a pace, carefully balancing a cup of tea.

PERCHIK. I've done John's tea, Mr Saul.

SAUL winks at him and puts his finger to his lips with a grin. He picks up the passport and waves it at PERCHIK, who freezes. He downs the tea.

VANESSA. Oh. Is John here? Only, I made these for him.

She takes a pair of knitted baby's booties from the pram. SAUL takes them and scrutinises them, brow furrowed. A long pause. He looks up.

SAUL. But, Vanessa! These are far too small!

VANESSA. Silly! They're not *for John*! They're for his *baby*!

VANESSA *and* SAUL *laugh their heads off at* SAUL'*s japery.*

(*Through giggles*.) Well? Where is he then?

SAUL (*still laughing too*). John? Oh, he was here. Yes. But he had to… head off.

SAUL *picks up the bucket and plonks it on the counter.* PERCHIK *stares at it.*

VANESSA. Oh. Never mind. I'll pop 'em down here for next time, eh?

VANESSA *bends behind the counter.* SAUL *stares at* PERCHIK*, nods at the bucket.*

SAUL. You might take another look at those accounts, Perchik. Ahem. (*He coughs into his hankie.*) Got anything for me, princess?

VANESSA *straightens.* SAUL *sits and leads her round the counter and onto his lap.*

VANESSA. Few bits and bobs. Too hot to carry on.

SAUL. Let's have a look then.

VANESSA. Couple of wallets. Nice cigarette lighter…

She starts to unpack the items from the pram. SAUL *snatches the lighter off her.*

SAUL. Naughty!

VANESSA. … three fags. And a lovely white loaf.

PERCHIK. Bread?

SAUL. She got bread! *Clever* gel!

He kisses VANESSA'*s cheek over and over.*

PERCHIK. Where d'you get all this?

VANESSA. Riots stopped for lunch. Lot of big queues about. (*Giggles*.) Get off, Saul! Dodgy Julio was up in Little Germany with a barrowload of old Christmas cakes. Easy to lift stuff during a scramble.

PERCHIK. You stole them, Vanessa?

SAUL. It's all by the book, of course. In the grandest of traditions.

VANESSA *puts the cigarettes in the fag cupboard.*

PERCHIK. What tradition would that be?

SAUL. She will only rob from the rich and only give to the poor.

PERCHIK. Oh. Right.

SAUL. Conveniently, we are the poor. Give him his watch back, Nessa.

PERCHIK. What? When did you – I never –

SAUL. She's extremely dextrous, ain't she? Taught her myself. Hours of training. I fully endorse women in the marketplace. Never let it be said I am not a feminist.

VANESSA. Saul is an excellent teacher.

SAUL. Now, wife, you'll have me blushing beetroot. Pop those in the safe, chop-chop.

VANESSA *takes the wallets and exits out back.*

PERCHIK. She's – That was incredible.

SAUL. Thank you. She's my greatest achievement.

PERCHIK. What d'you mean by that?

SAUL *coughs up some phlegm and spits it into his handkerchief.*

SAUL. Excuse me. The body must eject what it cannot entertain. Ha ha ha.

PERCHIK. Saul?

SAUL. I *mean*, Perchik, that I have *made her what she is*.

PERCHIK. And what's that then?

SAUL. One: the best pickpocket in Bradford. Two: more stupid than you could imagine. And three: not to be trusted.

PERCHIK. Is that not a bit daft? Making someone untrustworthy?

SAUL. Of course *I* can trust her. She's very loyal to *me*. Basically a labrador in a dress.

PERCHIK. Yeah, but who wants to marry a complete dog, right?

He laughs feebly. SAUL *stares at him.*

SAUL. A little… *conditioning* is very potent. Only through it will people accept your ways, clasp them to their odd little bosoms and, in time, become as you are.

PERCHIK. And what exactly is 'as you are'?

SAUL. Why! Culturally elite! The shop in which you stand, my dear little retard, is the last bastion of the greatest cultural machine the world has ever seen. We have civilised whole continents! Barbarous peoples and arid lands have been tamed by our touch!

PERCHIK. And modest with it, eh, Mr Saul?

SAUL. I couldn't expect you to understand, you porridge-sucking little Pict. Well, put this in your pipe and smoke it: do you know what 'poor Vanessa' did before I began work on her? She soaked her parents' sheets in kerosene and burnt them in their beds.

PERCHIK. Don't be daft.

SAUL. I don't think she realised what she was doing. Vanessa has always been one sausage short of a barbecue. That must be taken into account. But it was down to my testimony that her sentence / was suspended.

PERCHIK. Shut up –

SAUL. *I* rehabilitated her! If it weren't for my jurisdiction you'd have 'pyro' to add to the klepto-nympho-maniacal mix that is Vanessa's / psyche!

PERCHIK. I don't *believe* you!

SAUL. *Immaterial!* The gel is a fire hazard! That is an *empirical fact*. Why d'you think she's not allowed to light her own cigarettes, eh? You ever smelt burning flesh? It's not fragrant.

PERCHIK. She couldnay. They must've –

VANESSA *skips in, jauntily singing 'Blue Moon of Kentucky'. She takes the key and starts unlocking the cigarette cupboard.*

Ahhh!

SAUL. You're being rather cavalier with the fags of late, wife. Tell you what.

VANESSA *comes to him for a light.* SAUL *takes out his matches.*

You may have one if you can tell me what the adjective 'cavalier' means, Vanessa.

VANESSA (*sulkily*). I don't know, do I?

SAUL. It means 'showing a lack of proper concern'. See Perchik? To coin a phrase, '*Education, education, education.*' It's very important. She'd know that if she had it.

He lights a match, then blows it out and catches hold of her arm. It's bandaged at the wrist.

What's this, Nessa?

VANESSA. Oh that. S'nothing. Atifa again. What's-his-name, Mr Quasim's daughter. Said I was on her patch. That's never bloody her patch.

SAUL. Burn or cut?

VANESSA. Burn.

SAUL. It hurt?

VANESSA. Yeah. Stings a bit.

SAUL. You get her back, sweetheart?

VANESSA *shakes her head.* SAUL *kisses the bandage and puts the matches away.* VANESSA *is crestfallen.*

Never mind.

VANESSA. But –

SAUL. Run and fetch my hat and we shall pay a little visit to Miss Quasim.

He gives her a coin. She kisses him. He pats her on the bum and she exits to back. SAUL *takes a knife from the rack and sharpens it.*

PERCHIK. Hang on – What's goin' on?

SAUL. An eye for an eye, a tooth for a tooth. Or, for the secular audience who prefer the newest testament of all and hold the science of matter as their godhead, for every action, there is an equal and opposite reaction.

PERCHIK. Wha'?

SAUL. Revenge, Perchik! Nobody burns my wife and gets away with it!

PERCHIK. Except you, / ay?

SAUL. Except m – shut up.

PERCHIK. But you're no' leavin' me here on my own?

SAUL (*chuckling*). Let me tell you something, little Perchik. I have a dream. A dream – that one day, everything will be *exactly as it is now*.

PERCHIK. Well, you're an ambitious man, that's only natural.

SAUL. But I'm old, Perchik.

PERCHIK. Nonsense, Mr Saul. You're only as old as the woman you feel. Right?

SAUL. Well, she's old too. And when I'm gone I expect she'll do the decent thing.

PERCHIK (*hopefully*). Remarry, you mean?

SAUL. No, die. It would be unseemly for her not to. And then where will my Empire be? I need an *heir*. Do you see where I'm heading?

PERCHIK. Ay. Do you want to adopt me?

SAUL. Don't be disgusting. No. I have a better plan. This afternoon, little Perchik, you shall enter the world of commerce – not as a dogsbody… but as a *store manager*!

PERCHIK. An' that's good, is it?

SAUL. Yes.

PERCHIK. Oh.

SAUL. I knew you'd be excited! You are now In Charge, Perchik. I am *handing over the reins*! As my father did to me! The future of his Empire is in your hands!

PERCHIK. You want me to mind the shop? On my own? But we've no stock.

SAUL. No stock? Nonsense! We've got enough to last us a week! (*He bangs the bucket with his stick.*) Think what I'm offering you, Perchik! Promotion! Power! Prestige!

PERCHIK. Prestige?

SAUL. Well, no, not prestige, exactly. And not really power, actually. But certainly promotion! At least on a trial basis. Don't bugger it up.

VANESSA *enters.* SAUL *chucks* WINSTON's *suit at* PERCHIK, *who catches it.*

Make yourself respectable. (*He bangs the bucket again.*) And don't sell all that at once! Come on, wife. If you're very good I'll pinch you a Christmas cake on the way home.

SAUL *takes his panama hat from* VANESSA, *puts it on and exits.*

PERCHIK. But, Mr Saul! You don't want me to… I mean, I don't know how to…

VANESSA *follows* SAUL, *but drops her shawl.* PERCHIK *darts forward and picks it up.* VANESSA *takes it from him, flustered, and exits.* PERCHIK *surveys the shop.*

A store manager, eh? A *Store. Manager.*

He puts the suit on. It's too big for him. He pushes up his sleeves, and tentatively lifts a lump of meat out of the bucket. He drops it with a grimace on the counter. Raises the cleaver.

Bloody hell.

He brings the cleaver down with force and splits the meat in two.

Scene Two

Sundowner time. PERCHIK *is counting yen. The sack remains onstage.*

PERCHIK. ... Fifty, sixty, seventy, / eighty, ninety, a hundred –

> VANESSA *enters, cooling herself with the fan, nibbling on a Christmas cake.*

VANESSA. Phew. I'm sweating like a – Perchik? Where d'you get that from?

PERCHIK. I got it from *paying customers*, Vanessa!

VANESSA. You never! (*Beat.*) What they pay for then?

PERCHIK. For meat, my darlin'! Where's Saul?

VANESSA. He's just bringing the petrol in from the van. What meat?

PERCHIK. Oh, er – just some bits and bobs that came in with John.

VANESSA. You clever boy! The cottage'll be done in no time at this rate! Pack your bags, Perchik! We're off to the seaside!

> *She seizes his hands and they polka madly.* PERCHIK *pulls away.*

PERCHIK. Vanessa? I, um – I got you a present. On my lunch break.

> *He gives her a newspaper-wrapped parcel. She unwraps it. It's a book.*

VANESSA. What's this? *Lady Hamilton and Horatio Nelson: Behind Closed Doors.*

PERCHIK. Thought you might, you know... be interested.

VANESSA. Oh, it's *lovely*, Perchik.

> *She flicks through. Then looks up. A guilty smile. Faux nonchalance.*

Did you... um... Did you happen to see the sequel, Perchik?

PERCHIK. You mean the sequel to –

VANESSA. Yes.

PERCHIK *grins. He puts his hand inside his shirt. They fall into position.*

PERCHIK. 'I've come to fix your pianoforte, Lady Hamilton.'

VANESSA. 'Again, Lord Nelson?'

PERCHIK. 'Your G-string is a disgrace to the Empire and demands to be tuned.'

VANESSA. 'Oh! You've caught me in my scanties again! Once might be considered a mishap, twice is simply *asking* for a raping!'

PERCHIK. 'I make it my duty never to refuse a lady's request.'

VANESSA. 'Lord Nelson! Your britches are bulging like billy-o!'

PERCHIK. 'Well observed, you cum-hungry wench! They were designed by Princess Caroline of Brunswick herself to show off my every contour!'

VANESSA. 'Then God bless Princess Caroline of Brunswick!'

PERCHIK. 'And all who sail in her!'

PERCHIK *leans* VANESSA *over his knee as before.*

VANESSA (*whispering*). Perchik, don't –

But PERCHIK *leans in closer. This time,* VANESSA *does too.*

(*Whispering.*) You smell of the snow, you know. Cold has this – *scent* of its own. Like lemons squeezed over turpentine… I miss snow. Don't you…?

PERCHIK *nods. Their faces move closer.* SAUL *enters, carrying a petrol can.* PERCHIK *drops* VANESSA *on the floor with a thud.*

SAUL. Could you be more careful with my wife, Perchik? Her head may look like it is carved from a lump of igneous rock, but I assure you it will sustain only the lightest of batterings.

PERCHIK. Mr Saul! Look! Smell it! Smell that money, Mr Saul!

VANESSA. For the cottage, Saul!

SAUL. Yes, dear. For the cottage.

VANESSA. How many bastard bricks is that, Saul?

SAUL surveys the empty counter. Picks up a book from on top.

SAUL. What is this?

VANESSA. I bet it's loads!

PERCHIK. It's a book, Mr Saul.

SAUL (*incredulously*). *The Beginnner's Guide to Halal Butchery*?

VANESSA. I don't think I've ever been happier than I am right now.

PERCHIK. I just thought – you need to appeal to your core market.

SAUL. Perchik, could I have a word please? Over here?

PERCHIK. Yes, Mr Saul?

SAUL. I'm not quite sure how to put this, but… where is all of the meat?

Beat. PERCHIK *falters.*

PERCHIK. Well… I sold it. Didn't I? That's how I got the money. See?

SAUL (*trying to hold his temper*). But I told you not to sell it all at once, Perchik.

PERCHIK. But – I thought you were / joking –

SAUL. How am I supposed to expand my Empire if I've got to be tending to this scrawny little concern the whole time? That was s'posed to last us the week! You know how hard it is for me to get good stock! How did you shift it anyway?

PERCHIK. Ah! Now I know you're gonna love this, Mr Saul! I realised, what you need, is *publicity*! So I created an *advertising campaign*!

SAUL. Advertising campaign, Perchik?

PERCHIK. Well – I made a banner.

He unfurls a tatty banner, beautifully painted in an art-nouveau style, reading: 'MEET (for sale)'.

SAUL. Are you trying to tell me how to run my business?

PERCHIK. No! No, I wasn't trying to – I thought you'd be pleased!

SAUL. This is mutiny! You're trying to disrupt the equilibrium of my Empire!

PERCHIK. No, Mr Saul – I'm just trying to change – to improve –

SAUL. 'Improve'? On my father's legacy? I've got an idea, Perchik, let's you and me put on our Sunday best, drive to his resting place and have a good old dance on his grave together! Let's you and me do the bloody Macarena over my dead dad's body! Shall we? You little locust, I'll – *What the hell is this?*

SAUL picks up a small round object from the counter. A haggis.

PERCHIK. Umm. It's a haggis, Mr Saul.

SAUL. I beg your pardon?

PERCHIK. A haggis. Thought you could broaden your product range. Cater to new markets.

SAUL advances on PERCHIK.

SAUL. CATER TO NEW –

The telephone rings. All heads turn in that direction. A long pause. Then:

VANESSA. Shall I get that?

SAUL. Does anyone ever telephone you, wife?

VANESSA. No, Saul.

SAUL. Then is there any point in you getting it?

VANESSA. No, Saul.

SAUL. No, wife. There is not. I'll take it upstairs. This (*He shakes the haggis at* PERCHIK.) is an *outrage*. Stay where you are. Don't move a *muscle*.

SAUL exits. After a moment, the phone stops ringing.

PERCHIK. What's his fucking problem!

VANESSA. He just likes things done his way.

PERCHIK. But his way's *shite*!

VANESSA. He used to be a great man, Perchik. He just finds it difficult to *adjust*. He's shrunk a bit, you see. But men do shrink as they get old, don't they?

PERCHIK (*surly*). Yeah. They do. (*Beat.*) Except for their ears.

VANESSA. What?

PERCHIK. Well, they've always got really big ears, haven't they? Old men. Cos they carry on growing when everything else stops. So their ears are just *massive* –

SAUL *enters, fired up.*

SAUL. All the better to hear you with!

VANESSA. Saul!

SAUL. They've done it! They've finally gone and done it. Bastards!

VANESSA. Oh, Saul! Was that –

SAUL. Yes. Vanessa?

VANESSA. Yes, Saul?

SAUL. The map!

VANESSA. The map!

PERCHIK. What map?

SAUL. *The* map!

　　VANESSA *pulls down a huge roller blind.*

PERCHIK. WHAT MAP?

SAUL. THIS MAP.

On the blind is an enormous world map, like those found in Victorian schoolrooms. Britain is a small lozenge-shaped pink blob with two protrusions at the bottom right (Central London) and left (Cornwall). The rest of it is either eroded by sea (blue) or shaded in a different colour. Scotland is an island separated from England by Hadrian's Channel. SAUL examines it wistfully.

I remember when all this was pink.

PERCHIK. What's going on?

SAUL. Shut your mouth, garbage.

VANESSA. There, there, darling. Don't upset yourself.

SAUL. Oh, I know, I know. It had to happen. It had to go.

PERCHIK. What had to happen?

SAUL. But I still can't believe it. Gone. Just like that.

PERCHIK. Can someone tell me *what* exactly has gone?

SAUL. Cornwall. Bring me my pigments, Vanessa.

VANESSA fetches them.

PERCHIK. What do you mean, Cornwall's gone?

SAUL (*imitating in a whiny voice*). 'What do you mean, Cornwall's gone?' – Sold! I mean, it's been sold, you little tumour!

PERCHIK. Sold? *Sold?* Who have they sold it to?

SAUL. Who d'you think! The septic tanks and the Chinese got into bed together!

SAUL colours in Cornwall on the map with a black pencil.

It's not right. Remember that glorious holiday, yachting in Penzance, wife?

VANESSA. Camping, dear. In Torquay.

SAUL. We paddled in the sea and ate fish and chips.

VANESSA. It rained for a week. Lovely.

SAUL. There. Now, wife. If you wouldn't mind?

VANESSA nods solemnly, and pulls out a bugle. She stands to attention next to the map and plays a mournful 'Last Post'. SAUL salutes. He notices PERCHIK slouching.

Have you no respect?

He forces PERCHIK's arm up and watches VANESSA play, transported.

She may be riddled with herpes but her omberture is magnificent.

VANESSA finishes, and chokes back a sob.

No tears, wife. No tears. We shall fight the good fight. Even as the lights go out all over Truro, we shall keep the home fires burning.

He hands out black armbands to each of them.

VANESSA. It *was* a lovely service, wasn't it?

SAUL. It was, wife.

VANESSA. What Cornwall would have wanted.

SAUL. Yes, wife.

VANESSA. Don't you think, Perchik?

SAUL. Leave the boy, wife. He's in a state of mourning.

PERCHIK. No, I'm not.

SAUL. Yes, you are.

PERCHIK. No. I'm not!

SAUL. Yes, you are. I say you are!

PERCHIK. NO, I'M NOT!

SAUL. WELL, WHY NOT!?

SAUL *grabs a large knife and stabs it into the haggis and pushes it against* PERCHIK'*s throat.* PERCHIK *grabs the haggis off the knife and throws it at the map. It bursts. The contents of a sheep's stomach slither down the Empire.* VANESSA *inhales sharply.* SAUL *stares at the map. He slowly turns to* PERCHIK.

PERCHIK (*trying to divert the storm*). Oh, now, Mr Saul, I didnay mean to… Let's all just calm down, take a deep breath and –

SAUL (*quietly*). Get out.

PERCHIK. What?

SAUL. GET OUT!

PERCHIK. You cannay chuck me out! It's murder out there! Or prison, Mr Saul!

SAUL. You wet your own bed. You can lie in the damp patch.

PERCHIK. Please, they'll peel my kneecaps off – I didnay mean –

SAUL. I am not a *charity*.

PERCHIK. I spoke wrong, I *am* upset about Cornwall, I'm –

SAUL. I will not be *disrespected*.

PERCHIK. I'm proper devastated! And what about my wages?

SAUL. What wages? Do you know how much you cost me? It all adds up. And you don't care about money. / Remember?

PERCHIK. Please, Mr Saul!

SAUL. The matter isn't up for debate!

VANESSA. Please, Saul, let him stay! Please let him –

SAUL. Fine! One last chance. Sing 'Jerusalem', Perchik. Sing it all the way through.

PERCHIK. I can't – I don't / remember…

SAUL. SING!

PERCHIK (*singing*). 'And did those feet, in ancient times, walk upon England's pastures green… and did the – and did the – AND DID THE…'

SAUL. Wife.

PERCHIK. No, wait, I know it, it's ' – and did the – '

SAUL. Wife?

VANESSA. No, Saul, please –

PERCHIK. 'Countenance divine'? S'that it? 'Countenance divine'!

SAUL. *Wife*.

He smacks his stick against the counter. VANESSA *runs behind the counter, returning with a bottle of chloroform and a cloth. She puts it over* PERCHIK'*s mouth.*

VANESSA (*whispering*). I'm so sorry, Perchik.

PERCHIK *passes out.* VANESSA *opens the shop door. She and* SAUL *drag* PERCHIK *out.* SAUL *grabs* PERCHIK'*s bag and slings it. He slams the door and locks it behind him.* VANESSA *is weeping.* SAUL *pats her with the end of his stick.*

SAUL. There, there, wife. You mustn't get so *attached* to these boys.

VANESSA. How many has it been now? Is it seven? Or eight?

SAUL. You just can't get the staff.

VANESSA. We have such bad luck, don't we, Saul? Either they have to leave. Like Perchik. Or Stavros. Or they have an accident. Like Frankie. Or Klaus.

SAUL. I told you, wife. Klaus didn't have an accident. Klaus was headhunted by the International Monetary Fund.

VANESSA (*wailing*). He couldn't even add up on his fingers, Saul!

SAUL. The International Monetary Fund are admirably committed to a policy of equal opportunity, Vanessa.

SAUL suddenly bangs his stick in frustration.

Why don't people *listen* to me any more? Why won't they do as they're told!

VANESSA. Calm down, dearest.

SAUL. I'm sorry, wife. It's just – I liked that one. I really. I really quite liked that one.

VANESSA. Then let him stay! It's not too late.

SAUL. Yes, it is. He has betrayed my trust! I mean, there are *rules*, Vanessa. Protocol. An order of things. (*Beat.*) I'm so tired, wife. I feel like I'm being eaten at.

VANESSA. Poor Saul. (*She suddenly bursts into tears.*) Oh, I'm sorry, love. S'just, sometimes I think I'm being punished. For being such a wicked girl.

SAUL. Oh, *Vanessa*.

He chuckles fondly and puts his arms round her. He sighs.

You probably are.

VANESSA *bawls harder.*

Come on, wife. Buck up. Give me a kiss.

He puts a coin into her hand and she kisses him, still sniffing a bit.

All better?

She nods. He gives her the handkerchief. She blows her nose. He takes it back again.

Goodnight, wife.

He starts to exit. Then turns.

Vanessa? Do you think. Do you think I'm. Out of date?

VANESSA (*snottily*). Out of date, dear? Like a yoghurt, you mean?

SAUL. Yes, wife. Like a yoghurt. I sometimes wonder – no. Never mind.

SAUL *exits.* VANESSA *calls after him, drying her face.*

VANESSA. I don't think city living is good for you, my love. You'll feel better when we move to the cottage. Where it's nice. By the sea. Quiet. Just you and me. And Perchik.

SAUL (*off*). Not Perchik!

VANESSA (*sadly*). No. Not Perchik.

VANESSA *sits. She takes out the picture of the cottage. Traces a finger over it. Then puts it away, unlocks the fag cupboard and takes one. Realises she needs a light.*

(*Whisper to back.*) Saul? Saul? Are you there? Saul? Please? I need you to –

The letterbox creaks open and PERCHIK*'s hand appears through it, holding a lighter. He sparks it.* VANESSA *turns to see it, then runs to the door and leans into the flame.*

(*Whispering*). Perchik! What are you doing?

PERCHIK. Bleeding internally.

VANESSA. I / meant –

PERCHIK. I left something. In the icebox. For you.

VANESSA. For me?

PERCHIK. Yeah. It's a portrait.

VANESSA. Of me?

VANESSA *goes to the icebox.*

PERCHIK. Aye of you, you daft girl. Behind the bacon slicer!

She returns with a canvas. It's a portrait of a luminous version of VANESSA*'s genetically superior – if imaginary – sister.* VANESSA *examines it.*

VANESSA. Oh, Perchik…

PERCHIK. Do you like it?

VANESSA. It's lovely, Perchik. Only…

PERCHIK. Only what?

VANESSA. Only. It doesn't really look like me, does it?

PERCHIK. Let me in? I want to say goodbye. Proper, like.

VANESSA. I can't.

PERCHIK. Please?

VANESSA. No. Go away.

PERCHIK (*loudly*). 'Lady Hamilton! Your pianoforte is – '

VANESSA. Shh! Alright! Alright.

VANESSA opens the door. PERCHIK bursts in.

PERCHIK. Come with me.

VANESSA. Don't be stupid.

PERCHIK. Why? This place is a dump! Why would you want to stay here –

VANESSA. Maybe… because I'm just too stupid to leave.

PERCHIK. No, you're not. You just act like you are.

VANESSA (*smiles*). Well. There are certain advantages.

PERCHIK. To what?

VANESSA. To people thinking you're stupid.

PERCHIK. And what would those be then?

VANESSA. They're more surprised when you steal the watch off their wrist. (*Beat.*) I can't leave him, Perchik. He's –

SAUL (*off*). Vanessa!

VANESSA *hides her fag*. PERCHIK *ducks behind the counter.*
SAUL *enters.*

Are you coming up, Nessa?

VANESSA. In a minute.

SAUL. Your breathing doesn't sound too good tonight, love.

VANESSA. Just a bit tight. Nighty-night, Saul.

SAUL. Turn the lights out before you come up, eh?

SAUL exits. VANESSA *breathes a sigh of relief, before, a
second later, his head appears round the door again. She freezes.*

By the way. Um. I forgot. What with all the upset, but...

Beat.

Happy birthday, wife.

Beat. VANESSA *rises and kisses* SAUL *on the cheek. He grabs
her, needily rather than violently, and kisses her on the mouth.
She lets him. As they part, he puts something into her hand. It's
a tacky snow globe. She shakes it.*

It's, ah. It's for the cottage.

VANESSA (*touched*). Thank you, Saul. It's lovely.

SAUL (*embarrassed*). Wasn't very expensive.

VANESSA. It's *lovely*. Go to bed now, eh? I'll be up in a minute.

SAUL nods, exits. PERCHIK *emerges.* VANESSA *clamps a
hand over his mouth and listens till she hears the bedsprings
creak overhead. She moves her hand.*

See. He needs me. And I couldn't get by without him.

PERCHIK. That's just what he's told you. You said it yourself.
You're not stupid.

VANESSA. Oh, but I am. Awful thick.

She holds up PERCHIK's *belt, which she's managed to steal
without him noticing. He grins.*

PERCHIK. You thieving little –

VANESSA. You have to go now.

PERCHIK. He's never going to leave here, you know. (*Beat*.) I said, he's never going to –

VANESSA. You don't know what you're talking about, shut up –

PERCHIK. F'this place was mine I'd sell it tomorrow. You could be waiting another ten years. Longer. You could be stuck here / for the rest of your –

VANESSA. I'm sorry, Perchik. I've made up my mind. Goodbye.

PERCHIK. – life, no – *no*. Stay there. I've – I've got a – present. For you.

VANESSA (*new interest*). A present?

PERCHIK. Ay. A present. Y'never said it was your birthday. Dinnay move.

VANESSA. Perchik, I've got to –

PERCHIK. Close your eyes. Tight. (*Beat*.) Do it!

She sighs and closes her eyes. He's stumped for a moment. Then he spots his pillow. He peels off her shawl.

Right. Right. Okaaay. So. Imagine it's the past. Imagine it's the year… 2008. It's, um – Christmas Eve. You're on a train from Glasgow to Oban. When you get out at the –

VANESSA. How did I get to Glasgow?

PERCHIK. What?

VANESSA. I just like to get the details straight.

PERCHIK. I dunno. You hitched.

VANESSA. Hitched! For goodness' sakes, Perchik! A woman on her own! Hitching! I'd be dead in a ditch before Carlisle!

PERCHIK. Hitched a lift with a minibus full of nuns can I continue?

He guides VANESSA *in front of the counter and climbs onto it with the pillow.*

When you get out at the station you taste the sea straight away and the wind whips off the water and slashes at your face, it's that cold. From there you get on this huge ferry. As the boat travels onwards, the tide looks like it's made of tar because dusk is already falling and by the time you reach an island called Colonsay it's pitch black. And it's freezing now, you can't feel your feet in your boots so you hitch a lift in a truck driven by an eighty-six-year-old man with a tattoo of Johnny Cash on the back of his neck. He's playing a cassette tape of Tammy Wynette songs –

VANESSA. My favourite!

PERCHIK. Exactly – and singing along in a voice like cracked leather as he slugs whisky from a tartan thermos.

VANESSA. Cracked leather?

PERCHIK. I'm on a roll, don't interrupt. He drops you off outside a wee brick cottage on the edge of a white cliff –

VANESSA. Does the cottage have a room just for boots?

PERCHIK. It does. You don't go inside the cottage, not just yet, instead you scramble down the steep stony path to the shore below, and you stand on the beach, and hurl off your shoes to dip your toes in the icy Pacific, and the Northern Lights play in the sky, and the seaweed slimes under your feet and your ears pound with the cold, and you close your eyes to remember the feeling better when suddenly, then, at that moment, the chill in the air drops another half a degree, and from the clouds hanging over the ocean, something very strange, and very beautiful, and very cold, starts to happen…

PERCHIK *rips open the pillow. It's full of white down. He takes* VANESSA*'s electric fan and throws handfuls of feathers into the air, blowing them with the fan.*

And you open your eyes…

VANESSA *opens her eyes and gasps in delight. The feathers are falling. A clear, pure tone cuts through the air like a tuning fork.*

VANESSA (*whispering*). It's snowing. Perchik…

VANESSA *grins and shuts her eyes tight again.*

It's snowing.

PERCHIK. Are you cold?

VANESSA. Oh yes. I'm freezing. I'm absolutely…

PERCHIK. Really, really cold?

VANESSA. Yes! Yes!

PERCHIK. Can you smell it?

VANESSA. Yes!

> PERCHIK *jumps down from the counter. She grabs him.*

Have you got a pound, Perchik?

He shakes his head. She pulls him to her.

Never mind. You can start a tab.

> *She kisses him. They kiss again, and again, their embrace getting more and more heated, an itch being scratched.* PERCHIK *lifts her up and sits her on the counter.*

(*Dreamily.*) Do you know what I'd like? I'd like for this whole shop to just disappear as if it was never there in the first place. Imagine it.

PERCHIK. The blaze of an Empire going up in flames, ay?

VANESSA. And then we could live in the cottage by the sea… you and me… in the cottage by the sea… and Saul can be a snowman…

> *They fall back to kissing. There's a creak overhead.* VANESSA *looks up.*

Come on. Let's go.

PERCHIK. Now?

VANESSA. Yes, Perchik. Now.

SAUL (*off*). Vanessa?

> VANESSA *jumps off the counter and runs to the icebox. Her shawl catches in the door.* PERCHIK *jumps behind the counter.* SAUL *enters. Goes to the icebox door.*

Vanessa? Please come to bed. I. I can't sleep.

> *He waits. No answer. He sighs. He looks small, sad and tired. He exits out to the back. A beat, then* PERCHIK *creeps out. He spots the painting, picks it up.*

PERCHIK (*whispering*). Vanessa? Vanessa?

He waits. Looks searchingly round the shop. Then spots the shawl trapped in the door of the icebox. He smiles. Goes over and whispers through the door.

Vanessa, I'm going now. But I'll come back tomorrow. Promise. Won't be long now. We'll have you paddling in the sea before pancake day, ay? Vanessa?

SAUL *enters from the back, silently. He is holding a raised shotgun that is pointed at* PERCHIK's *head. He stalks towards him with glee.*

The thing is… I think – I might – sort of – be in love with you.

As SAUL *speaks,* PERCHIK *starts and spins round.*

SAUL. That's very flattering, Perchik. But you're really not my type. Can I see your passport, please?

PERCHIK. I – I – I don't have a passport, Saul.

SAUL. No?

Beat. SAUL *cocks the gun and grins.*

Oh dear.

Blackout. Gunshot.

End of Act Two.

Interval.

ACT THREE

'Evacuation'

PERCHIK *has been hung upside down from a butcher's hook by a rope tied round his ankles. He is gagged and writhing. The gunshot at the end of Act Two was aimed at his right foot, and this is now a bloody bundle.* SAUL *sits, reading a newspaper.*

PERCHIK. Mmmmrggrhh!

SAUL. How many times, Perchik? Like this: The rein in Spein falls meinly on the *plein*. It's not *hard*. Now try *agein*.

PERCHIK. Mmmmmmmrrrgggghhh!

SAUL. Better! Much better! We'll make a newsreader of you yet.

PERCHIK. Mmmmmmrrrrrrrrrgggggggghhhhhhh!

SAUL. On the contrary, I don't think I'm being at all unreasonable. You've put my business in jeopardy. You've trespassed on my property. And now this monstrosity!

He produces the painting of VANESSA *and holds it up.*

PERCHIK. Ret ri row!

SAUL. Stop mumbling, Perchik, it's tiresome. What? What's that?

He pulls the gag off PERCHIK*'s mouth.*

PERCHIK. Let me down!

SAUL. No. You have hurt me greatly with this tomfoolery. You come in here, stealing my jobs –

PERCHIK. You *gave* me the job.

SAUL. Semantics, Perchik! Say you're sorry.

PERCHIK. No! I think I need a doctor.

SAUL. Where are your manners?

PERCHIK. You shot me in the foot!

SAUL. It was just a joke, Perchik! You have to *laugh*, don't you? Now say you're sorry.

PERCHIK. Fuck off!

SAUL. Oh dear. I think I'll make a telephone call.

He goes to the phone and lifts the receiver.

Let me see. Nine. (*He dials.*) Nine – (*He dials, then pauses.*) Now, what was the last bit?

He goes behind the counter, pulls out a telephone directory and looks it up.

Ah yes. (*He returns to the phone.*) Nine. Yes, hello, police please. (*Beat.*) Ah, hello, yes, I'm calling with information regarding a dangerous artist who is On The Loose.

PERCHIK. Saul…

SAUL. Yes. Yes – armed, dangerous *and* Scottish. Yes, his name is –

PERCHIK. Okay!

SAUL (*to* PERCHIK). I'm on the telephone. It's very rude to interrupt.

PERCHIK. I said okay! I'll say it.

SAUL surveys him for a second, then turns back to the phone.

SAUL. Oh, I *am* sorry. I've made a mistake. I was trying to get hold of my mother but I've just remembered she's dead. Goodbye. (*He hangs up.*) Well?

PERCHIK. I'm – sorry.

SAUL. Good! And I forgive you! See how simple that was? And to show there are no hard feelings, I've cooked you a special dinner. A pork chop, Perchik!

He brings a plate out from behind the counter.

PERCHIK. I can't eat that.

SAUL. Oh, but you can. The dental plan of the human mouth is perfectly equipped for you to eat it. Eat it.

He cuts it up for PERCHIK *and puts the fork to his face.*

PERCHIK. Don't make me.

SAUL. Who holds the matches, Perchik?

PERCHIK. You do, you do, but please, I'll be sick –

SAUL. Don't make Sauly hold your nose.

SAUL forces a forkful into PERCHIK*'s mouth and waits for him to chew.*

Chew.

Pause.

Chew and be grateful.

PERCHIK *chews, gagging as he does.*

Now swallow.

He swallows. SAUL *claps his hands in delight, then starts to cut* PERCHIK *down.*

It's terribly clever, don't you think, for the human body to allow the bolus – that is, the chewed sustenance – to contradict physical science. The swallow is an action that should by rights be impossible when suspended upside down. And yet the contraction of the muscles in peristalsis propels it upwards in flagrant defiance of the universal laws of gravity. It wants to get to the stomach so very much, you see. It's almost enough to make you believe in God, isn't it? Was that good? Bearing in mind the trouble I took, would you say that it was a very tasty dish?

PERCHIK *is finally down. He nods.*

Good! Good, I'm so glad.

SAUL *spits into a handkerchief.* PERCHIK *makes a painful run for the door.*

No you don't.

He grabs PERCHIK *and perches him on the counter.*

You can't just run away from your responsibilities. Come on now, you've barely touched your chop.

PERCHIK. I'm full.

SAUL *feeds him another mouthful.*

SAUL. Here comes the aeroplane into mouthy airport, wooo…

Now, what would you say if I was to tell you that this juicy pork chop had come from a very *special* sort of pig? It is the kind of pig that the natives of the Marquesas Islands of Polynesia refer to by the name of 'long pig', but which civilised society – people who have trains and washing machines and a ninety-nine per cent literacy rate – the kind of pig that they refer to as… Vanessa. What would you say to that, eh?

PERCHIK *spits it out*.

Don't waste food! Don't waste my wife! Remember her with your stomach. The memory in the brain is unreliable, it paints in black and white. If you want the truth of the woman that was Vanessa, see what she does to your duodenum!

PERCHIK. What've you done to her? You're disgusting. You sick old –

SAUL. Don't say that! I loved her! Even if she was common and trampy / I still –

PERCHIK. I'm gonnay call the police.

SAUL. – *loved her* – no! You mustn't, promise me you won't – it was an accident. She must've still been in the icebox. I locked the door but I didn't know she was still in there, I swear. And then, when I came down this morning – the *shock*, Perchik. Later, when you were still unconscious I mean, I thawed her out. Her lashes were all crystalled with frost and her skin – alabaster, that's what they call it, isn't it?

PERCHIK (*sourly*). I thought you didnay allow poetry in the shop.

SAUL. Allowances are made on days of mourning, Perchik! Allowances are made!

PERCHIK. Oh God. Poor Vanessa…

SAUL. Why are you getting upset? She was my wife! Do you know what I did next?

PERCHIK. I don't want to know.

SAUL. I laid her on the marble and performed the last rites.

PERCHIK. You're no' religious, Saul. You're a hypocrite as well as a murderer.

SAUL. Not the last rites of the soul. The last rites one might perform on a hundred-pound pig. I laid her on the slab and I butchered her.

PERCHIK. No...

SAUL. *Yes.* I took my sharpest knife and slit her, throat to belly. Then I removed the head with my saw, such care I took, except the blood, Perchik. The blood was awful – Vanessa's juices all over my hands. I made the slits behind the Achilles tendons, inserted the gambrel – the gambrel, Perchik, is a frame from which we hang the beast – and up she went. I removed her arms. And then I skinned her.

PERCHIK. I'm think I'm going to be sick.

He runs behind the counter and heaves.

SAUL. An incision through the belly to remove the guts, being especially careful with the intestines for they can contaminate the meat and render it unfit for eating.

PERCHIK. You're lying, aren't you? I mean. You couldn't do that. Not even you, this is –

SAUL. I did it, Perchik! Believe me, I did it! And I put the radio on and listened to *The Archers* omnibus *while* I did it!

PERCHIK. Animal!

SAUL. I was mad with grief!

PERCHIK (*sarcastically*). Is that right?

SAUL. Of course! Otherwise I would never have been able to skin my wife or listen to *The Archers* omnibus! (*Beat.*) It was sawing the feet off that was hardest, Perchik.

PERCHIK. Oh God.

SAUL. I always loved my wife's feet, her breeding showed in her feet, but I had to do that so that I could deal with the rear ham, didn't I? Then I separated ribs from chops and trimmed the loin, cutting out the bundles of muscle with my smallest knife. And with love, Perchik. With such love.

PERCHIK. You didn't love her, you killed her! Don't pretend to me that you loved her!

SAUL. Of course I loved her! I lived with her, didn't I? She was my best chum… It was an accident, Perchik, I promise. I wanted her inside me, so I could remember her. Physically. I ate her heart. Fried it and ate it with my fingers and I felt so warm inside. You know how I hate seeing food go to waste. Oh God. Vanessa.

SAUL *breaks down, wretched, and lies heaving, sobbing on the floor.*

PERCHIK. Saul?

Pause. PERCHIK *pulls off the restraints on his hands.*

Saul? Get up! You disgusting piece a… I'm gonnay fuckin' kill you – I'm gonnay –

VANESSA *hurriedly enters the shop.* SAUL *sits up slowly, enjoying the look on* PERCHIK*'s face, and his sobs transform into laughter, relishing his trick.*

Vanessa? You – But he told me he'd –

SAUL. He thought I'd *eaten* you! Ha! He actually thought I'd eaten you, old girl! / He's awful gullible!

PERCHIK. You bastard. You sick, inhuman –

SAUL. You stupid goose! I wouldn't waste the good knives on her!

VANESSA. I did it. I said I would and I did. I went to the police and I told them.

SAUL (*laughing*). Eh? What d'you tell 'em then? You mad old sow. I bet they had a good old laugh at you, didn't they?

VANESSA. Yes. They laughed at me. At first. But then I told them some other things and they stopped laughing and they turned a little tape recorder on and asked if I'd like a cup of tea.

SAUL. And what you did tell them?

VANESSA. I said yes please. Two sugars.

PERCHIK. He meant –

VANESSA. I know what he meant. I told them how he sits on my lungs and how he boxes my ears and how he tattooed his name on my bum and it went septic and how he put Frankie in the cement mixer and how you put Detective Prawn in a sack and how you don't have planning permission for the extension / of your Empire –

SAUL. You little bitch. You ungrateful slut. Telling everyone our business. That's our private, secret business!

VANESSA. I just want things to *change* around here – cos I warned you, Saul. I warned you to let him go or I would and you didn't *listen*, / so you've only yourself to blame.

SAUL. I didn't think you'd actually do it, did I?!

VANESSA. Maybe they'll give you a talking-to you'll take mind of, / cos God help us you don't listen to me any more.

SAUL. After all I've done for you, telling people things like that! Our secrets, state secrets, this is *treason*, you know what happens to traitors? Is this your idea, Perchik?

VANESSA. No! It wasn't him. It wasn't his idea. Don't –

SAUL. Remember who holds the matches here, you two. I could burn you both in your beds. This shop is a tinderbox, the walls in here are little more than parchment.

VANESSA. It wasn't him!

SAUL. I don't believe you.

VANESSA. It wasn't!

SAUL. Well, who was it then? Who's the dozy sod who'd put up with you for –

VANESSA. He's a poet. He lives in a big house that looks like a bride cake. He imports tropical fruit, he hates Elgar, his mum's a Hindu, he doesn't eat meat and – and – he's *French*.

SAUL. You lying little *bitch*.

He punches her in the stomach. She doubles over. PERCHIK *jumps on* SAUL'*s back.*

PERCHIK. Don't touch her! You touch her again and I'll kill you!

SAUL. You? You couldn't maim a monkey.

PERCHIK. Don't touch her!

VANESSA. It's alright, Perchik, leave off.

SAUL. I wouldn't sully my hands with her! She's no better than that sack of old horse. Past her sell-by-date and reeking of rot.

He throws PERCHIK *off, runs to the counter, grabs his cleaver.*

Do you know what they do in the Arab lands to promiscuous women who can't keep their knickers on? They cut off their hands! Think what a saving you'll make on gloves, wife!

VANESSA. No, Saul, please, put it down, put it down. PUT IT DOWN!

PERCHIK. Saul, calm down, please, come on now, let's just –

SAUL. Mr Everard! To people like you my name is Mr Everard! Get me a pen, Perchik. I want to write a label for my wife. I'm posting you to France, girl. Get in there.

He drags VANESSA *towards the sack.*

VANESSA. No! Get off!

SAUL. Bon voyage, you little cow!

DIXON (*off*). Open up.

SAUL. Who the bloody hell is that?

DOCK (*off*). It's the police!

PERCHIK. It's the police.

VANESSA. They must have followed me here. I didn't think…

SAUL. Well, that makes a change, doesn't it? You *silly* stupid mare. You really have surpassed yourself this time! Your mistakes have already cost me the best years of my life and two kids, was that not enough for you, eh –

VANESSA (*whiplash venom*). Oh, I hope you rot in a windowless cell, you vicious grasping nasty old *cripple*.

SAUL *gasps then freezes as if he's been slapped.* VANESSA *freezes too, both surprised by what she has said. Finally* SAUL *makes a tiny, frail noise.* VANESSA *runs to him and cradles his head, trying to soothe him. He whimpers as she rocks him.*

Saul, I'm *sorry*. I'm sorry, love. I didn't / mean –

SAUL. You hurt my feelings!

VANESSA. I spoke without thinking –

SAUL (*whining*). You're not playing *nice* tonight, Vanessa!

VANESSA. I got carried away. Shh… it's alright… shh…

PERCHIK. Vanessa…

SAUL. You're not playing *nice*.

There's more banging on the door.

PERCHIK. Vanessa, he was gonnay cut your hands off!

DIXON (*off*). We have here a warrant for the arrest of a Mr Saul
Everard –

DOCK (*off*). – regarding the disappearances of Detective Derek
Prawn, John Grimmup, Francesco Mancini, and various other
charges of a serious nature.

SAUL. They're going to arrest me? But this is my Empire. They
can't arrest me.

VANESSA. I think they can, my love. Help him, Perchik!

PERCHIK. You've got to be kidding!

VANESSA. Please? *Please?*

PERCHIK *sighs.*

PERCHIK (*gesturing to the sack*). Hide in here, Saul.

SAUL. No!

PERCHIK. Get in the sack. Quickly, or do you want to go to prison?

SAUL. I can't! It's full of maggots. You'll tell 'em, won't you,
Nessa, tell them it was lies and I never did none of those things?
You'll tell them, sweetheart, won't you?

VANESSA. Course I will, I'll tell them it was all lies.

PERCHIK. Won't matter if she does. They all heard her. They had
a little tape recorder.

VANESSA. Oh, what have I done? I'm sorry, my love. I didn't
mean –

DIXON (*off*). Mr Everard? If you don't open this door we shall break it down.

SAUL. Pigs!

PERCHIK. Get in the sack, Saul.

SAUL. Can't. Sick.

PERCHIK. I'm sorry?

SAUL. I'll be sick.

PERCHIK. So be sick. Get in the sack.

SAUL. I see your game! You want to pack me off to France! Well, I won't go! I won't!

PERCHIK tries to guide SAUL to the sack. SAUL sobs help-lessly. All defences down.

Please… please don't make me… I can't. I'm frightened.

PERCHIK. Of what?

SAUL. … I don't know.

VANESSA (*softly*). It's for your own safety, Saul.

DIXON (*off*). I'm going to give you from the count of ten…

VANESSA. Come on, Saul. Quick!

DOCK (*off*). This is your last warning. Get ready, Dixon. / Ten, nine, eight, seven, six, five, four, three, two, one…

PERCHIK. Get in, Saul.

As DOCK counts down, PERCHIK manhandles SAUL in. SAUL is dazed. He grabs hold of PERCHIK's hand desperately.

SAUL (*faintly*). Your fingers, Perchik… or the pies?

PERCHIK pushes SAUL's head in and closes the sack. SAUL's stick clatters to the floor. DOCK reaches 'one' and the POLICEMEN burst in.

PERCHIK. Hello, gentlemen.

DIXON. Is this the residence of Saul Everard?

DOCK. That's my line, Dixon.

DIXON. Does it matter?

DOCK. No, it doesn't matter, it's just, you know, you have your
lines and I have my lines, but whatever. You've said it now.

DIXON. Well, you can say it again.

DOCK. I'm not going to say it aga –

DIXON. Fine. Is this the resi –

DOCK (*very fast, to get it out first*). Isthistheresidenceof-
SaulEverard?

PERCHIK. I've never heard of a Mr Everard. Have you, Tammy?
(*Beat.*) Tammy?

VANESSA. No. I've never heard of nobody.

DIXON. Excuse me, ma'am, but you *were* the lady down at the
station this morning?

PERCHIK. What an idea! Imagine, my wife – common-law, mind
– in a police station! Sat amongst a load of junkies and gigolos!
She's been here with me all day. Building a coal shed. For our
coal. I'm afraid you've had a wasted trip, but while you're here,
this is a sack of black-market offal. I'd take it away and incin-
erate it if I was you.

VANESSA. Perchik, no.

PERCHIK. Crawling with maggots. It's a public-health
disturbance.

VANESSA. I said *no*, Perchik.

DOCK. Well, that's quite an order, sir, but it begs some questions,
don't it.

DIXON. It certainly does beg some questions.

VANESSA. Please, Perchik. *Please*.

DOCK. Such as, how did you come by this *offal*, if I may ask?

DIXON. And he may.

PERCHIK. Don't threaten me. It was got –

VANESSA. Don't say anything.

PERCHIK. It was procured on the request of your Chief, but he failed to collect it. If you take us down we'll take half the West Yorkshire police force with us and you won't be very popular at the Christmas party. Think of the media frenzy, Officer. A very black picture it would paint of the boys in blue. I can see it now. 'Maggotgate.'

VANESSA. Perchik –

DOCK. 'Maggot – '?

PERCHIK. Gate.

DIXON. Are you attempting to blackmail us, sir?

DOCK. Be quiet, Dixon. 'Maggotgate.' Dear me. Not a pretty picture. Our apologies, sir, we'll be getting along now. Dixon.

DIXON. Dock!

DOCK. *Dixon.*

They face each other off. DIXON *breaks first.*

DIXON. Right. If you say so. My apologies.

The POLICEMEN *start to move the sack. Coming to,* SAUL *starts to shout.*

SAUL. Put me down! I'm not going to France! You hear me, I won't go!

The two POLICEMEN *freeze and exchange a look.*

DIXON. The offal appears to be – talking. Sir.

PERCHIK. Well, they are very highly evolved maggots, Officer.

Pause.

DIXON. Very good, sir.

He tries to proceed, but DOCK *stays rooted to the spot.*

DOCK. Big?

DIXON. Come on, Dock.

PERCHIK. Sorry, pal?

DIXON. He's not your pal.

DOCK. I'm not your pal. These maggots. Are they big?

PERCHIK. Big? Oh yeah. They'll have your arm off.

DOCK. Hmmm.

Beat. Then DOCK *thoughtfully pulls out his gun and shoots the sack. It goes quiet.*

There's a long silence, finally broken by DOCK.

As you were, Dixon.

DIXON. What's all this, 'as you were'?! You're not in the army, how many times?

DOCK. Could be in the army. Just don't want to.

DIXON. Oh yeah. I forgot. They were just playing hard-to-get when they turned you down. Twice. Your feet are flatter than your sister's chest and you can't shoot for shit.

DOCK. I shot that alright, didn't I?

DIXON. That's the other thing, always shooting everything, bang bang bang. You've got to hold your *fire*, mate.

DOCK. I'm not your mate.

DIXON. Dock! After all we've been through together!

DOCK. Shut up. We'll talk about this in the car.

DIXON. All I'm saying is, you didn't have to shoot a sack of meat what's already dead.

DOCK. Did you want to listen to that racket all the way to the municipal dump? It was giving me gip, Dixon. Much like you are now. Can we go?

PERCHIK *holds the door open, and* DOCK *and* DIXON *exit with the sack.*

DIXON (*exiting*). You're trigger-happy, that's what you are.

PERCHIK *slams the door after them. He hobbles excitedly to* VANESSA.

PERCHIK. Did you see me? Did you see that, Vanessa!

VANESSA. Perchik –

PERCHIK. They were all, 'Are you trying to bribe us, sir?'

VANESSA. Perchik –

PERCHIK. And I was all, 'Take that, pigs!' And – And – Vanessa?

VANESSA *starts to bawl*.

Hey hey hey, what's this? Come on darlin' – shhh.

He puts his arms round her and kisses her on the head.

It's alright. Don't cry, pet. It's all over. He'll not hurt you any more.

VANESSA. You put him in a sack!

PERCHIK. I was just trying to help him. You asked me to –

VANESSA. Do you think they'll – I mean, they can't. They won't –

PERCHIK. Oh, I think they will, darlin'. They will. This country is lucky to be served by the most efficient police force in the world.

VANESSA. If I go after them, it might not be too late.

PERCHIK. Say what you like about them but they *get the job done*.

VANESSA. He should have a proper burial.

PERCHIK. It's too late, darlin'.

VANESSA. Decent. In the ground. With flowers.

PERCHIK. They'll be miles away by now.

VANESSA. Singing 'Jerusalem'.

PERCHIK. And it's not safe out there.

VANESSA. I'd like to mourn him properly. In a traditional fashion.

VANESSA *goes to exit by the front door.*

PERCHIK. Vanessa…

VANESSA. It's not right.

PERCHIK. I said *no*, sweetheart.

He slams the door. VANESSA *runs to the icebox.*

Come on, darlin'. I know you're upset but – Aw, *Jesus*.

VANESSA *stops, closes the door.* PERCHIK *flinches in acute pain as he stands on his bad foot. He spots* SAUL*'s stick on the floor. He picks it up and tries it. He likes it.*

VANESSA. You should see a doctor about that foot.

PERCHIK. Yeah, yeah. I know. Jus' – give us a minute to think, okay, love? Would you like a banana?

VANESSA. What?

PERCHIK. *Would you like a banana?*

VANESSA. Oh. Yeah. Ta.

He gets two bananas from his bag and they eat quietly.

You know, I never wanted to marry a butcher. I hate this shop.

PERCHIK. I know what you mean.

VANESSA. Really?

PERCHIK. I'm a vegetarian.

They look at each other. A beat. Then they laugh. Another pause.

VANESSA. See, this is nice, isn't it? This is nice. Quiet. Bananas. I mean, I wish you hadn't done it, Perchik. He didn't have long left in him, you see. I was just going to let him go gently. Fade away. I wouldn't have jumped the gun myself.

PERCHIK. So to speak.

VANESSA. But now he's gone anyway... we can start again, can't we? Do it properly. A new era.

PERCHIK. Yeah, that's right – a new Empire.

VANESSA. That's not what I / said –

PERCHIK. You don't really mind, do you, darlin'? About Saul?

VANESSA. Oh yes. I do. I feel awful.

VANESSA *goes to open the cigarette cupboard.*

PERCHIK. Well, you shouldn't, my love. 'The body must reject what it cannot entertain', eh? What just happened was just the evacuation of a toxin. Speaking of which – maybe you should lay off those a bit, eh? Apparently they're no' very good for you.

VANESSA. *But, Perchik –

PERCHIK. *New start, Vanessa! Chance to get rid of all those bad old habits, eh? (*He picks up the painting of* VANESSA.) Tell you what, you give up that and I'll give up painting monstrosities like this, eh?

He laughs. Then VANESSA *does too. She takes a deep breath. Then she smiles.*

VANESSA. Yeah. Yeah. Okay. Deal.

She picks up PERCHIK*'s knapsack with purpose, and hands it to him.*

Come on then. Let's go.

PERCHIK. Give us a minute, darlin'! I'm beat. And there's no rush is there?

JOHN JUNIOR *enters, empty-handed.*

JOHN JUNIOR. 'Livery!

PERCHIK. John Junior! What a treat. Come in, come in.

JOHN JUNIOR. Meat.

PERCHIK. I'm sorry?

JOHN JUNIOR. I have with me here a delivery of meat.

PERCHIK. Ah! (*Beat.*) Where?

JOHN JUNIOR *looks round. Then he leans out the door and yells.*

JOHN JUNIOR. John Junior Junior! Stir your stumps, boy!

JOHN JUNIOR JUNIOR *enters, hot and sweaty, carrying a sack.*

JOHN JUNIOR JUNIOR. What about this weather, eh?

PERCHIK. What about it?

JOHN JUNIOR. John Junior Junior, this is our esteemed customer, Mr Everard.

PERCHIK. Ah, Mr Everard's not – I mean, he isn't – I, er –

(*Beat.*) Call me Saul, John Junior. Thank you. Just put it down there.

JOHN JUNIOR JUNIOR. Meat.

JOHN JUNIOR. Compliments of the boss.

PERCHIK. Ay. I should think so.

JOHN JUNIOR *pulls out a letter and clears his throat.*

JOHN JUNIOR. He give me something to read: 'Dear Mr Everard comma please accept my apologies for the recent customer product interface error full stop the ano – ano – '

JOHN JUNIOR *holds the paper out for* JOHN JUNIOR JUNIOR *to read.*

JOHN JUNIOR JUNIOR. Anomaly.

JOHN JUNIOR. '– was the result of a systems failure and the problem has now been rectified.' So that's that.

PERCHIK. Tell your boss that... Tell him that his sentiments are appreciated and I look forward to continuing our longstanding commercial relationship.

JOHN JUNIOR. Er. Yeah. Same time tomorrow, Mr Everard?

PERCHIK. Ay. Same time tomorrow, fellas.

They exit. PERCHIK *opens the sack.* VANESSA *stares at him.*

Now that's fresh, Vanessa!

VANESSA. They thought you were –

PERCHIK. This'll fly off the shelves!

VANESSA. You said you were –

PERCHIK. Turn this place around in no time.

VANESSA. But we don't need it now, do we?

PERCHIK. Well...

VANESSA. We're not staying. You didn't think... We're not staying.

Pause.

PERCHIK. See, I've been thinking, Vanessa, and what it is, is I've come to the conclusion that leaving the shop would not be a financially sound decision.

VANESSA. But that's what you said! This place is a dump, / you said!

PERCHIK. Only needs a lick of paint, a few… cosmetic enhancements.

VANESSA. But what about your story? The sea, the cottage –

PERCHIK. We could make a killing.

VANESSA. Our plans?

PERCHIK. I've got responsibilities now.

VANESSA. But you *said* –

PERCHIK. I've never been a man of property.

VANESSA. We could start again.

PERCHIK. The expansion out back's nearly finished.

VANESSA. Start differently –

PERCHIK. I've got big plans for it.

VANESSA. Evolve.

PERCHIK. No.

VANESSA. Yes!

PERCHIK. Darlin' –

VANESSA. We were s'posed to *leave*. We were s'posed to go to the cottage.

PERCHIK. I don't think you fully / understand our –

VANESSA. Go to the cottage in the country –

PERCHIK (*exploding*). THERE IS NO COTTAGE, YOU STUPID – !

Beat.

VANESSA. What?

PERCHIK. There's no cottage. He cut the picture out of a magazine.

VANESSA. Out of a… No. No, I don't think…

VANESSA *takes the picture out and unfolds it slowly.*

PERCHIK. Ay. Out the *Sunday Times* Style section.

PERCHIK *takes the picture out of her hand and flips it over.*

D'you never think why there was an advert for pain-free leg-waxing on the other side, ye daft girl? Jesus, hon. You really are thick, aren't you?

VANESSA. I don't know. I never… And you knew this? All along?

PERCHIK. Didn't want to piss on your bonfire, did I? It was a nice idea, like.

VANESSA. So we're stuck here.

PERCHIK. Not stuck, darlin'! Look at this place! Why would we want to go somewhere new when we have all this?

PERCHIK *pulls down his banner, clears the books, and chucks the haggis remains.*

VANESSA. Why go somewhere new when…

PERCHIK. Just need to clear this rubbish and we'll get ourselves back to normal, ay?

VANESSA. *I want to paddle in the sea, Perchik!*

PERCHIK. There's time for paddling, darlin'! Once things have calmed down a bit. Give it a couple of months, a year or two. Be patient, eh?

VANESSA. I've been *patient*. / For ten years I've been very, very –

PERCHIK. Let's vote on it, ay? All those in favour say yay.

VANESSA. – PATIENT. Nay. I'm sorry, Perchik.

PERCHIK. Yay. Motion carried. What for?

VANESSA. I'm not staying here. I can't. I'll go mad.

PERCHIK. Aw, you're jus' tired, lamb.

VANESSA. And I told you not to do it. It wasn't right.

PERCHIK. He was a toxin, Vanessa!

VANESSA. One mustn't bite the hand that feeds one, 'ticularly in this day and age.

PERCHIK. Vanessa!

She spins to face him – furious, frustrated.

VANESSA. And now I'm *stuck* here. With nothing but a load of old meat and *you*!

PERCHIK. But – I *love* you.

VANESSA. Yes. I dare say you do.

Pause. VANESSA *examines* PERCHIK.

(*Brightly.*) Never mind, eh? I'm really doing you a favour. You wouldn't last a minute where I'm going. You're a vegetarian.

PERCHIK. What?

VANESSA. Survival of the fattest, love. There's just not enough substance in a banana.

PERCHIK *puts his arms around her and kisses her neck. Wheedling.*

PERCHIK. But… Lady Hamilton… if you leave me, who's gonnay fix your pianoforte?

He puts a hand under her skirt.

VANESSA. Stop it. I read that book you gave me, Perchik. I read the whole thing. You know what happened to Lady Hamilton? She *died*. In prison. In Calais, Perchik. Her skin went all yellow and she lost her memory and her hair fell out and then she *died*. She never had a powdered wig or nothing. Poor cow.

PERCHIK. Vanessa, what the fuck are you talking about?

VANESSA. Meanwhile, old Horatio Cyclops gets a state funeral! Well, no thank you. (*Beat. Idea.*) I'll tell them you was a hero, Perchik.

She starts to undress, calmly, down to her slip.

PERCHIK. Tell who?

VANESSA. A martyr. I'll say you rescued me from my bed, averting your eyes as you carried me down so as not to hurt my modesty, dressed as I was in only my *scanties*.

PERCHIK. Stop talking shite.

VANESSA. And then, *cavalier* in regard for your own young life, you plunged yourself back into the raging fire to attend to the old man who was still snoring while his Empire went up in flames, before finally choking to death on the *fragrant smoke* of his burning flesh, as it drifted up into the big brown canopy of Bradford's *halitosis skies*.

PERCHIK. I've had enough ay this. I'm going to bed. You comin'?

VANESSA. *These are the new rules, Perchik.* You better pay attention. I'm going to paint the pictures from now on. And I'm not playing any more silly games.

She swiftly produces a pair of handcuffs, locks one end on PERCHIK*'s wrist and locks the other end onto the counter. He tries to pull them off. He can't.*

PERCHIK. What the – Where d'you get these from?

VANESSA. Dixon. Or Dock. Can't remember which.

PERCHIK. Okay. So joke's over, get 'em off me. Now!

VANESSA. He was a great man. Once. It's a shame you had to pick up only his worst habits. Do you see?

PERCHIK. No, I fuckin' don't!

VANESSA. Well. Never mind. I'll tell them you were a hero.

PERCHIK. Ay, and I'll tell them you're a cracked bitch. Get 'em off me!

VANESSA *rummages in* PERCHIK*'s bag. Pulls out a half-litre bottle of clear liquid.*

VANESSA. Oh, I don't need speaking for. I've got a tongue of my own. What's this?

PERCHIK. S'white spirit. Turps. For my brushes. / Vanessa –

VANESSA. Lovely.

She starts to douse the area behind PERCHIK *with the contents of the bottle, singing a few bars of 'Blue Moon of Kentucky' as she does so. He strains to see.*

PERCHIK. What are you doing? I swear, darlin', I'm gonnay count to ten –

VANESSA. The thing is, Perchik, this shop… it's a veritable tinderbox…

PERCHIK. Don't start that again. Give us the key. S'cutting into /
my wrists –

VANESSA. A tinderbox, Perchik. The walls are little more than
parchment.

She pulls out a matchbox and shakes it.

PERCHIK. Vanessa – eh, Vanessa, no!

VANESSA. I stole them from his pocket.

PERCHIK. Vanessa! You dare – / *you dare* –

VANESSA. I'm sorry, Perchik. I can't understand what you're
saying. I'm ever so stupid.

VANESSA *takes a pair of scissors and cuts the ribbon on the
key. She unlocks the cupboard and takes a cigarette, sticks it in
her mouth.*

PERCHIK. Vanessa, darlin', please, whatever you're – Please.
Please!

VANESSA. Poor thing. Look at you. You're terrified.

VANESSA *lights a match and uses it to light the cigarette.
Takes a drag.*

Good.

She throws the lit match. Blackout.

PERCHIK. VANESSA!

Tammy Wynette's 'Stand by Your Man' plays.

*The music stops. The lights come up. The sounds of waves
breaking and gulls calling.* VANESSA *is at the seaside. She
takes off her shoes and socks, tucks her skirt into her knickers,
and steps forward into the cold water. She smiles. The light
fades as she paddles up the shore.*

The End.